Tolley's Practical Guide to the Working Time Directive and Regulations

by

Michael Grisenthwaite

and

Carole Grant-Garwood

of

Deloitte & Touche

Tolley Publishing Company Limited

A member of the Reed Elsevier plc group

Whilst every care has been taken to ensure the accuracy of the contents of this work, no responsibility for loss occasioned to any person acting or refraining from action as a result of any statement in it can be accepted by any of the authors, editors or the publishers.

Published by
Tolley Publishing Company Limited
2 Addiscombe Road
Croydon Surrey CR9 5AF England
0181-686 9141

Printed in Great Britain by
Hobbs the Printers, Hampshire

List of Contributors

Carole Grant-Garwood LLB(Hons), Barrister

Michael Grisenthwaite LLB(Hons), LLM, Solicitor

Biographies

Carole and Michael are both senior managers with Deloitte & Touche.

Carole was called to the Bar in 1991.

Michael qualified as a solicitor in 1993.

Both Michael and Carole have been working in employment law since qualifying.

PREFACE

The aim of this book is to provide an overview of, and a practical guide to, the *Working Time Regulations 1998*. This is a very new piece of legislation, which contains some wide definitions. In the absence of any judicial interpretation, it is not possible to provide a definitive interpretation. What is provided, however, is a view as to the likely interpretation. As such, it should not be relied upon, in any particular circumstance, as a substitute for proper professional advice.

Acknowledgement must go to Alison Haynes and Catriona McIntyre without whose support and assistance this book could not have been written.

Contents

Chapter   *Page*

1 – Introduction

Aims and Objectives   21
Studies   21
Other Working Time Legislation   22
Working Time in the United Kingdom   22
Working Time in EU Member States   23
The European Directives   24
Challenging the Directive   25
The Cost of Compliance   26
Implementing the Directive – Consultation Papers   26
Interpretation of the Directive   27

2 – Scope

To Whom do the Regulations Apply?   29
Workers Working Outside Great Britain   29
Scope of the Directive   30
Scope of the Regulations   31
'Employees'   31
The 'Control' Test   32
The 'Integration' Test   32
Tools and Equipment   32
Mutual Obligation   33
The 'Personal Service' Test   33
The 'In Business on His/Her Own Account' Test   33
The 'Multiple' Test   34
The Terms of the Contract   34
Payment   35
Premises   36
A Balance of Factors   36
'Workers'   37
Delegation   37
Conditions   38
Self-Employed Individuals   38
Services Through a Company   39
Young Workers   39
Agency Workers   40
Trainees   42
Crown Employment   42
Armed Forces   43
House of Lords Staff   43
House of Commons Staff   44
Police Service   44
Agricultural Workers   45
Employer   46

3 – Exclusions and Exceptions

Introduction   47
Exclusions   47
    Armed Forces and Civil Protection Services   48
    Medical Practitioners   48
    Young Workers   48
The Future of the Exclusions   49
    Seafarers   49
    Doctors in Training   50
Scope of the Exclusions   51
    Determining Involvement in Excluded Sector   51
Exceptions   53
    Domestic Servants   53
    Workers on Unmeasured Working Time   54
    Other Special Cases   56
       Workers Who Travel a Long Way to Work   57
       Security and Surveillance Activities   58
       Continuity of Service   58
       Surges in Activity   59
       'Force Majeure'   59
    Young Workers Employed on Ships   60
    Workers in the Armed Forces   61

4 – Working Time

What is 'Working Time'?   62
Definition of Working Time   62
    Employees 'On Call'   63
    Lunch Breaks   64
    Travelling   64
    Working From Home   65
    Work-Related Activities   66
    Statutory Rights to Time Off   66
    Working Abroad   67
Relevant Training   67
Relevant Agreements   68
Records   69
Record-Keeping Arrangements   69

5 – Rights and Obligations

Introduction   70
Obligations   70
Maximum Weekly Working Time   70
    Employers' Duties   71
    Reference Period   71
       Amending the Reference Period   72
    Calculating the Average Hours Worked   73
       Excluded Days   73
       Example Calculations   74
    Agreement to Exclude the Maximum Working Week   75

Record-Keeping Requirements	76
Blanket Agreements	77
Duration of the Agreement	77
Limits on Hours	78
Pressure to Enter Agreements	78
Work for Other Employers	79
Provisions Relating to Night Work	**80**
Night Time	81
Definition of a Night Worker	81
Reference Period	83
Workers 'On Call' At Night	83
Limit on Night Work	84
Reference Period	84
'Normal' Hours	84
Calculating the Average for Night Work	85
Example Calculations	86
Work of Special Hazards	87
What is 'Work Involving Special Hazards'	88
Exceptions	88
Reduction in Pay	89
Health Assessments	90
Young Workers	90
Carrying Out the Health Assessment	91
Frequency of Assessment	93
Disclosing the Results of Assessment	93
Transfer of Night Workers to Day Work	93
Failure to Find Alternative Work	94
Duty to Make Reasonable Adjustments	94
Young Workers	95
Agreements to Amend or Modify the Provisions	95
Records	**96**
Patterns of Work	**96**
Entitlements	**98**
Interaction of the Entitlements	98
Rest Periods	**99**
Daily Rest	100
Shift Workers	100
Weekly Rest Period	101
Calculting the Rest Period	102
Young Workers	102
Shift Workers	102
Rest Breaks	**103**
When to Take the Break	103
What Constitutes a 'Break'?	104
Collective and Workforce Agreements	104
Determining When the Entitlement Arises	104
Pay for Rest Breaks	105
Entitlement to Annual Leave	**105**
Excluded Workers	105
'Leave Years'	106
Agricultural Workers	106
Pay in Lieu of Leave	106
Bank and Public Holidays	107
New Workers	107

Contents

Entitlement to Leave – What is a Week?   108
  Part-Time Workers   109
Dates on Which Leave May be Taken   111
  Giving Notice   111
    Agricultural Workers – Notice   112
Failure to Provide Entitlement   112
Payment for Periods of Leave   112
  Determining a Week's Pay   113
    Overtime   113
    Shift Workers   113
    Amount of Remuneration   114
    Piece Workers   114
    Workers With No Normal Hours   114
Termination   **115**
Amount to be Paid on Termination   115

6 – Agreements to Modify or Exclude the Provisions

Excluding or Modifying the Limits   **117**
  Which Agreement to Use   117
Individual Agreements   **118**
  Bringing an Agreement to an End   119
  Current contracts   119
Relevant Agreements   **120**
Collective Agreements   **121**
Workforce Agreements   **121**
  Employee Representatives   122
  When to Use a Workforce Agreement   122
  Workforce and Collective Agreements   123
  Formal Requirements   123
  Elected Representatives   125
  Number of Representatives   125
    Eligible Employees   126
    Excluding Candidates   126
    Protection of Candidates   127
    Other Purposes   127
    Voting Rights   127
Compensatory Rest   **128**

7 – Enforcement, Offences and Remedies

Enforcing the Regulations   **129**
Enforcement – the HSE and Local Authorities   **129**
  Scope of the Enforcing Powers   131
  Inspectors' Powers   131
  Restrictions on Inspectors' Powers   132
  Employer Offences   133
  Penalties   133
  Who Can be Prosecuted/Fined?   134
Enforcement – Employment Tribunals   **134**
Worker's Complaint – Regulation 30   **135**
  Time Limits for Regulation 30   136

Armed Forces   136
Out of Time Complaints   137
Remedies for Regulation 30   137
Heads of Compensation   138
Holiday Pay in Lieu   138
The Right Not to Suffer Detriment   **139**
What is a 'Detriment'?   140
Termination of Contract   141
Compensation   142
Perceived Rights or Entitlements   142
Remedies for Suffering a Detriment   143
Mitigation of Loss   143
Time Limit for Claim of Suffering a Detriment   143
Unfair Dismissal   **144**
Automatic Unfair Dismissal   145
Assertion of a Statutory Right   **145**
Time Limit   146
Remedies for a Dismissal for Asserting a Statutory Right   146
Appeals   **147**
Civil Claims   **147**
Conciliation   **147**
Advisory, Conciliation and Arbitration Service (ACAS)   147
Restrictions on Contracting Out   148
Compromise Agreements   148
The Public Interest Disclosure Act 1998   **150**

Appendices

Summary of Provisions in the Regulations   152
Full and Partial Exemptions   156
Record-Keeping   159
Agreements to Exclude Provisions   160
European Working Time Directive   164
The Working Time Regulations 1998   177

Table of Statutes

Access to Medical Records
Act 1988   5.35

Agriculture Wages Act 1948
                                      2.30
s 17   2.30

Agriculture Wages (Scotland)
Act 1949   2.30

Air Force Act 1955
s 180   7.12

Army Act 1955
s 190   7.12

Courts and Legal Services
Act 1990   7.35

Disability Discrimination
Act 1995   5.36, 5.38, 6.16

Employment Rights Act
1996
                        2.2, 5.15, 7.25
s 45A   7.17, 7.18, 7.19,
                    7.21, 7.24, 7.35
     (1)   7.17
     (4)   7.19
s 48   7.22
     (3)   7.24
     (4)   7.24
     (1ZA)   7.17, 7.19
s 48A   7.24
s 49   7.22
     (5A)   7.19

s 98
     (1)(b)   5.30, 5.37
     (2)(d)   5.30
s 101A   7.19, 7.25, 7.26, 7.35
s 104   7.27, 7.28
     (2)   7.27
s 196   2.2
s 197   7.19
s 200   7.17
s 202   7.17
ss 221–224   5.72
s 221
     (2)   5.72
     (3)   5.76
s 222   5.74
s 230
     (1)   5.15, 5.24
     (3)   2.4, 2.29
s 234   5.24, 5.73
Part V   7.17
Part X   7.19

Employment Tribunals Act
1996
s 18   7.35
     (1)   7.33
     (2)   7.33
     (3)   7.33
s 21   7.30

Health and Safety at Work etc
Act 1974   1.3, 5.41, 7.2
s 2
     (1)   1.3, 5.14
     (2)   5.14
s 37   7.8

Industrial Relations Act 1971
Part IX   2.4

Merchant Shipping Act 1995
s 55(2)(b)   3.20

Naval Discipline Act 1957
s 130   7.12

Police Act 1997
s 9(1)(b)   2.29
s 55(1)(b)   2.29

Public Interest Disclosure Act 1998   7.36
s 43K   7.36

Reserve Forces Act 1996
Part XI   2.26

Trade Union and Labour Relations (Consolidation) Act 1992   6.9
s 5   6.7
s 178   6.7

Table of Statutory Instruments

Health and Safety (Consultation with Employees) Regulations 1996
(SI 1996/1513)   6.9, 6.18

Health and Safety (Display Screen Equipment) Regulations 1998
(SI 1998/2792)
Reg 4   1.3, 5.42, 5.52

Health and Safety (Enforcing Authority) Regulations 1998
(SI 1998/494)   7.2

Management of Health and Safety at Work Regulations 1992
(SI 1992/2051)   5.17, 5.33
Reg 3   5.28

Police Federation Regulations 1969 (SI 1969/1787)
Reg 7(3)   2.29

Police Federation (Scotland) Regulations 1985 (SI 1985/1531)
Reg 7(3)   2.29

Working Time Regulations 1998 (SI 1998/1833)
Reg 1(2)   2.2, 4.9
Reg 2(1)   .   2.4, 2.22, 2.23, 2.24,
                                          2.29, 2.31, 4.10, 4.11, 5.18,
                                                 5.19, 6.6, 6.7, 6.8
Regs 4–8   5.2
Reg 4
         (1)   3.12, 3.13, 5.3, 5.14,
                                                     5.24, 6.3, 6.5
         (2)   3.12, 3.13, 5.4, 5.16, 7.3
         (7)   5.8
Reg 5   5.11, 6.3, 7.34
         (2)
              (a)   6.3
              (b)   5.13, 6.4
         (3)   6.3
         (4)   5.11, 6.3

Working Time Regulations 1998 – continued
Reg 6
    (1) — 3.12, 3,13, 3.14, 5.22
    (2) — 3.12, 3.13, 3.14, 5.22, 7.3
    (6) — 5.24
    (7) — 3.12, 3.13, 3.14, 7.3
    (8) — 5.28
Reg 7 — 5.31
    (1) — 3.12, 5.41, 7.3
    (2) — 3.12, 3.20, 5.32, 5.41, 7.3
    (5)(b) — 5.35
    (6) — 3.12, 5.33, 5.36, 5.38, 7.3
Reg 8 — 3.12, 5.42, 7.3
Reg 9 — 4.12, 5.12, 5.41, 7.3
    (b) — 5.41
Reg 10 — 5.45
    (1) — 3.13, 3.14, 5.46, 7.10
    (2) — 3.19, 3.20, 3.21, 5.46, 7.10
    (3) — 5.46
Reg 11 — 5.45
    (1) — 3.13, 3.14, 7.10
    (2) — 3.13, 3.14, 7.10
    (3) — 3.20, 3.21, 7.10
    (4) — 5.49
    (6) — 5.49
    (7) — 5.44
    (8) — 5.50, 5.56
Reg 12 — 5.42
    (1) — 3.13, 3.14, 5.52, 7.10
    (2) — 5.55
    (3) — 5.52, 5.54
    (4) — 3.19, 3.20, 5.16, 5.52, 7.10
Regs 13–16 — 5.58
Reg 13 — 5.66
    (1) — 5.58, 5.60, 5.67, 7.10
    (2) — 5.58
    (6) — 5.60
    (7) — 5.64
    (8) — 5.64
    (9) — 5.62, 5.66
      (a) — 5.62
Reg 14 — 5.78
    (2) — 7.10, 7.16
    (4) — 5.79
Reg 15 — 5.67

Working Time Regulations 1998 – continued

Reg 16	5.66
(1)	7.10, 7.16
Reg 17	5.44
Reg 18	3.2
Regs 19–27	3.11
Reg 19	3.12, 5.29
Reg 20	5.3, 5.29
Reg 21	3.14, 5.5, 5.6, 5.29
(a)	3.15
(b)	3.16
(c)	3.17
(d)	3.18
(e)	3.19
Reg 22	
(1)	5.47
(b)	5.51
(c)	5.46
(2)	5.47
Reg 23(a)	6.20
Reg 24	6.20, 7.3, 7.10
(a)	5.47, 5.51
(b)	5.47, 5.51, 6.20
Reg 25	3.21
(3)	7.10
Reg 26	2.22, 3.20
Reg 27	2.22, 3.14, 3.19
(2)	7.10
Reg 28	7.2
(1)	7.3
(2)	7.2
(3)	7.2
Reg 29	2.25, 2.26
(1)	7.6
Reg 30	2.2, 2.27, 7.9, 7.14, 7.15, 7.33, 7.35
(1)	5.64, 7.10, 7.14
(2)(b)	7.13
(3)	7.14
Reg 30	
(4)	7.14
(5)	7.16
Reg 31	5.15, 7.9, 7.17, 7.19
(1)	7.17
(3)(b)	7.19
Reg 32	7.9, 7.19, 7.25
Reg 33	7.33
Reg 34	7.30

Working Time Regulations 1998 – continued

Reg 35		7.34
	(1)	6.1
	(3)	7.35
	(4)	7.35
	(5)	7.35
Reg 36		2.23
	(2)	2.23
Reg 37		
	(1)	2.25
	(2)	2.25
	(4)	2.25
Reg 38		2.26
	(2)	7.12
Reg 39		2.27
	(3)	2.27
Reg 40		2.28
	(4)	2.28
Reg 41	(1)	2.29
	(2)	2.29
	(3)	2.29
Reg 42		2.24
Reg 43		2.30
Sch 1		6.8, 6.9, 6.12
para 1(a)		6.12
	(b)	6.12
	(c)	6.12
	(d) (i)	6.12
	(ii)	6.12
	(e)	6.12
para 2		6.12
Sch 1		
para 3		6.13
	(b)	6.15
	(c)	6.16
	(d)	6.15, 6.19
	(e)	6.14, 6.19
	(f)	6.19
Sch 2		2.30
para 1(a)		5.61
Part II		5.1
Part III		3.1
Part IV		7.1

Table of EU Legislation

EC Treaty of Rome 1957
Art 118a   1.7, 1.8, 3.2
Art 100   1.7
Art 189(3)   1.10
Art 235   1.7

Framework Directive (89/391/EEC)   2.31, 3.2, 3.4
Art 2   2.3
Art 3   3.12
Art 6(2)(d)   5.42

Protection of Young People at Work Directive
(94/33/EC)   1.6, 2.22
Art 9.3   5.31
Art 10   5.45

Working Time Directive (93/104/EC)
Art 1   2.3
Art 2   4.2, 5.19
Art 3   5.43
Art 4   5.43, 5.52
Art 5   5.42
Art 6   5.3, 5.10
Art 7   5.43, 5.58
Art 8   5.22
      (1)   5.21
Art 9   5.31
Art 11   5.41
Art 12   5.17
Art 13   5.42
Art 16.2   5.5, 5.8
Art 17   3.11
Art 17.4   3.11
Art 18   5.10
Art 18.1(b)(ii)   5.58

Table of Cases

Airfix Footwear Limited v Cope [1978] ICR 1210   2.9

British Fuels Limited v Baxendale & Another and Wilson &
    Others v St Helen's Borough Council [1998] IRLR 706   1.10

Cameron v Royal London Ophthalmic Hospital
    [1940] 4 All ER   3.12
Carmichael v National Power plc The Times, 2 April 1998   2.9
Clark v Oxfordshire Health Authority [1998] IRLR 125   2.9
Commissioner of Police of the Metropolis v Lowrey-Nesbit
    EAT 952/97   2.29
Construction Industry Training Board v Labour Force Ltd
    [1970] 3 All ER 220   2.23

Johnstone v Bloomsbury Health Authority
    [1991] IRLR 118   5.14, 7.31
Jones v Tower Boot Co Ltd [1997] IRLR 168   4.5

Lee Ting Sang v Chung Chief-Keung (1) Shun Shing
    Construction & Engineering Co Ltd [1990] IRLR 236   2.16
Litster and Others v Forth Dry Dock & Engineering Co Ltd
    [1989] ICR 341   1.10

Marleasing SA v Commercial International De Alimentacion
    [1992] 1 CMLR 305   1.10
McMeechan v Secretary of State for Employment
    [1995] ICR 444   2.23

Norton Tool Co Ltd v Tewson [1973] 1 All ER 183   7.20

O'Kelly v Trusthouse Forte plc [1983] IRLR 369   2.9, 2.16
Ogle v Morgan 1 DGM   3.12

Re Junior Carlton Club [1992] 1 KB 166   3.12
Re Keilacott and others [1992] 1 KB 466   3.12
Re Selfridge & Co [1922] WN 241   3.12
Re Wilkinson [1992] 1 KB 584   3.12
Ready Mixed Concrete (South-East) Limited v Ministry of
    Pensions and National Insurance [1968] 1 All ER 433   2.6, 2.12

SIMAP v Conselleria de Sanidad y Consumo de la
Generalitat Valencia C–303/98   3.4, 4.3, 5.21

Stevenson Jordan & Harrison Limited v MacDonald and
Evans [1952] 1 TLR 101   2.7

United Kingdom v Court of the European Union 1997
Case C–84/94   1.2

Webb v EMO Air Cargo (UK) Ltd [1993] ICR 175   1.10

Yewens v Noaks (1880) 6 QBD 530   2.6

ABBREVIATIONS

DDA	*Disability Discrimination Act 1995*
DTI	Department of Trade and Industry
EAT	Employment Appeal Tribunal
ECJ	European Court of Justice
EC Treaty	European Communities *Treaty of Rome 1957*
ERA	*Employment Rights Act 1996*
EU	European Union
European Commission	European Commission of the European Union
European Council	European Council of Ministers
Framework Directive	*Council Directive No 89/391/EEC* of 12 June 1989 on the introduction of measures to encourage improvements in the health and safety of workers at work
Government	United Kingdom Government
guidance notes	The DTI's Guide to the Working Time Regulations
the Directive	*Council Directive No 93/104/EC* of 23 November 1993 concerning certain aspects of the organisation of working time
the Regulations	*Working Time Regulations 1998 (SI 1998/1833)*

the White Paper   *White Paper on Sectors and Activities Excluded from the Working Time Directive COM (97) 334 of 15 July 1997*

The first consultation document   *Measures to implement provisions of the EC Directive on the Organisation of Working Time,* March 1997

The second consultation document   *Measures to implement provisions of the EC Directives on the Organisation of Working Time and the Protection of Young People at Work,* April 1998

TULR(C)A   *Trade Union and Labour Relations (Consolidation) Act 1994*

1 – Introduction

Aims and Objectives [1.1]

The aim of this book is to provide an understanding of the *Working Time Regulations 1998* ('the Regulations') as far as it is possible to do so at present.

A number of areas of the Regulations will require clarification by the tribunals and courts in the United Kingdom and by the European Court of Justice. Therefore, at this stage it is only feasible to provide guidance on the possible interpretation of the Regulations.

The background to the Regulations, set in the context of their European origins, is considered below.

Studies [1.2]

There have been many studies and publications across Europe and around the World on work patterns and their effect upon the health of workers. As early as 1957, the International Labour Office in Geneva published an 'Introduction to Work Study' with a view to it being 'used all over the world'. The conclusion was that long working hours can cause accidents, illness and stress.

The European Court of Justice has stated that the scientific data appears:

> 'fully to justify, for reasons of protection of health and safety at work, the introduction of a set of rules intended generally to limit working time and reduce it to a minimum' (*United Kingdom v Court of the European Union 1997 Case C-84/94*).

To this extent, working time is a health and safety issue.

Working time and working patterns are also economic issues. A decline in the curve of production is often attributed to a worker's fatigue. Studies have shown that regular breaks in work increase the productivity of the worker (*The Hawthorne Studies* (1939) Harvard University Press). It is well recognised that workers who work for too long a period before taking a rest will incur 'excessive cumulative fatigue' (RM Curries 1972). For example, the long distance driver is regularly reminded by signs on the motorway to take a break, as tiredness can kill.

Other Working Time Legislation [1.3]

The Regulations are the first significant piece of legislation to regulate working time in the UK. Nevertheless, the concept of regulating working time is now a permanent feature of the British working environment.

General protections are afforded to employees by the *Health & Safety at Work etc Act 1974* (*HASAWA 1974*). Specifically, an employer is under a duty:

> 'to ensure, so far as is reasonably practicable, the health, safety and welfare at work of all his employees' (*section 2(1), Health & Safety at Work etc Act 1974*).

It is important to remember that these duties continue to exist alongside those duties found in the Regulations.

Specific protection is granted to VDU operators, who are not expected to sit at their screen all day with the only break being for lunch. This feature of our working practice comes from European legislation which has been implemented by *Regulation 4* of the *Health and Safety (Display Screen Equipment) Regulations (SI 1992/2792)* which provides as follows.

> 'Every employer shall so plan the activities of users at work in his/her undertaking that their daily work on display screen equipment is periodically interrupted by such breaks or changes of activity as reduce their workload at that equipment.'

Working Time in the United Kingdom [1.4]

It is well known that the United Kingdom has, within Europe, the highest percentage of employees working more than 48 hours per week. European studies confirm this fact.

The figures below show the percentage of full-time employees who work more than 48 hours each week (Eurostat 1994).

United Kingdom	22%
Belgium	3%
Denmark	7%
France	7%
Germany	6%
Greece	7%
Ireland	9%
Italy	4%
Luxembourg	4%
Netherlands	1%
Portugal	7%
Spain	4%

In addition, British people work the longest hours in Europe. On average, a British worker works 43.5 hours each week, yet the average elsewhere in Europe is 40.3 hours.

A recent survey (*New Earnings Survey 1996*) indicates that male manual workers in the UK are the largest group to work more than 48 hours each week.

	Men	Women
Manual	25.6%	8.6%
Non-manual	6.3%	1.6%

It is inevitable that, as the United Kingdom draws ever closer to the other Member States of the European Union, its laws and working practices will also grow closer.

Working Time in EU Member States [1.5]

To a British person, the concept of regulating working time is foreign. Certain United Kingdom laws touch upon the subject but there has been no specific legislation dedicated to regulating working time in a comprehensive manner before the Regulations came into force on 1 October 1998.

Other Member States of the EU had laws on working time before the EU introduced a Directive on the subject. In addition, the reluctance to regulate the hours a worker can be required to work in a week is not as strong in other EU Member States as it is in the UK. For example, the countries set out below all have a lesser maximum working week limit than the UK.

Country	Hours
Austria	40
Belgium	40
France	39
Netherlands	45
Spain	40
Sweden	40

In France, legislation introduced on 13 June 1998 reduced the current limit of 39 hours each week to 35 hours each week. This change will be brought in gradually. Employers of at least 20 employees must comply with the change from 1 January 1999. Employers of less than 20 employees must comply from 1 January 2002.

Whilst other Member States have statutes permitting a maximum working week of 48 hours, in practice the maximum is reduced to a lesser number of hours by collective agreement.

For example, in Germany, the statutory maximum is 48 hours but it is common to reduce this to between 35 and 40 hours each week by collective agreement.

The European Directives [1.6]

The idea of regulating working time is not an unusual concept for the majority of the Member States of the European Union. Therefore, the idea of having a European Directive which promotes a higher level of protection for the health and safety of workers in this area was anticipated.

The Regulations implement both the European *Working Time Directive (No 93/104/EC)* ('the Directive') and parts of the *Protection of Young People at Work Directive (Council Directive 94/33/EC 1994)*.

Whilst participating in the drafting of the Directive along with its European partners, the UK Government led the negotiations for significant opt-outs and derogations from parts of the Directive.

For example, the Directive provides workers with paid annual leave of four weeks but the Government negotiated annual leave of three weeks for an interim period.

This concession will end on 23 November 1999, when UK workers will be entitled to four weeks' paid annual leave.

Challenging the Directive [1.7]

Despite the Directive coming into existence from 23 November 1993, the UK Government decided to challenge its legitimacy under European law by taking a case to the European Court of Justice.

The basis of the claim was that the Directive was adopted as a health and safety measure under *Article 118a* of the EC *Treaty of Rome 1957*.

The principal aim of *Article 118a* is for Member States to:

> '... pay particular attention to encouraging improvements, especially in the working environment, as regards the health and safety of workers, and shall set as their objective the harmonisation of conditions in this area, while maintaining the improvements made'.

Any legislation introduced under *Article 118a* required only the approval of the Member States by qualified majority. This allowed the Directive to be adopted without the UK Government's approval.

The Government contended that the Directive should have been introduced under *Article 100* or *Article 235* of the EC Treaty. Either of these Articles require a unanimous decision by the Member States.

The Government argued further that the use of the words 'working environment', 'health' and 'safety' in *Article 118a* indicated that any legislation arising out of *Article 118a* should be limited to the physical conditions and risks at the workplace. If this argument was correct, then the Directive was unlawful, as it went too far by dealing with such matters as holiday leave.

The Court ruled that the Directive had been adopted correctly under *Article 118a* as a health and safety measure.

The Court made a number of rulings, including the following:

- ○ the use of the words 'working environment', 'health' and 'safety' should be given a broad interpretation;
- ○ where the principal aim of the measure in question is the protection of the health and safety of workers, *Article 118a* must be used;
- ○ it was not accepted that the essential objective of the Directive is to increase jobs and reduce unemployment, although it may have an impact in these areas; and
- ○ there are no grounds for annulling the Directive in its entirety.

One point was conceded, regarding weekly rest periods. The Court ruled that the connection between the health and safety of workers and the requirement that the weekly rest period 'shall in principle include Sunday' had not been established. Thus, this part of the Directive was annulled.

This was, therefore, a hollow victory for the UK Government.

The Cost of Compliance [1.8]

It is interesting to note that *Article 118a* of the EC Treaty, upon which the Directive is founded, provides that:

> 'such Directives shall avoid imposing administrative, financial and legal constraints in a way which would hold back the creation and development of small and medium sized undertakings'.

However, the DTI's consultation paper of April 1998 stated that the estimated cost of complying with health assessments for night workers in both public and private sectors will amount to £0.05 billion each year.

The total cost of compliance with the Regulations is estimated at £1.9 billion each year for British industry.

The European Commission is committed to reporting every five years on the application of the Directive in practice. Therefore, it is possible that changes may be made to the Directive in future amendments. The exclusions and exceptions in the Directive are being reviewed by the European Council and the European Commission.

Implementing the Directive – Consultation [1.9]

Following the European Court of Justice's ruling that the Directive was founded on the correct provision of the EC Treaty, the Government proceeded to consult both sides of industry.

On the 6 March 1997, the Government issued its *Consultation Document on Measures to Implement Provisions of the EC Directive on the Organisation of Working Time.*

Following the general election in 1997, the new Government issued a second public consultation paper in April 1998. This second paper included a draft of the proposed *Working Time Regulations*, which were later amended as a result of the consultation process.

Interpretation of the Directive [1.10]

The Directive continues to play an important role in implementing the Regulations. As with any European law, it is important to interpret UK legislation in the light of the European legislation that gave rise to it.

This principle was set out by the European Court of Justice in the case of *Marleasing SA v Commercial International De Alimentacion* [*1992*] *1 CMLR 305* which ruled that:

> 'in applying national law, whether the provisions in question were adopted before or after the Directive, the national court called upon to interpret it is required to do, so far as possible, in the light of the wording and the purpose of the Directive in order to achieve the result pursued by the latter and thereby comply with [*Article 189(3)* of the Treaty]'.

Where UK legislation has been passed to implement a European Directive, the House of Lords is willing to give an interpretation of the UK legislation which takes into account the purpose of that Directive.

This principle had already been demonstrated in the case of *Litster & Others v Forth Dry Dock & Engineering Co Ltd* [*1989*] *ICR 341*. The House of Lords inserted words into provisions of UK legislation which implemented a European Directive. The reason for this was to ensure that UK law was compatible with the European Directive which it purported to implement.

In the later case of *Webb v EMO Air Cargo (UK) Limited* [*1993*] *ICR 175*, the House of Lords clarified its view on interpreting UK law. The House of Lords stated that:

> '... it is for a UK court to construe domestic legislation in any field covered by a Community Directive so as to accord with the interpretation of the Directive as laid down by the European Court, *if that can be done without distorting the meaning of the domestic legislation*' (emphasis added).

This view has recently been reaffirmed by the House of Lords in *British Fuels Limited v Baxendale & Another and Wilson & Others v St Helen's Borough Council* [*1998*] *IRLR 706*.

Once the European Court of Justice begins to give its interpretation on matters arising out of working time, then UK courts and tribunals must interpret the Regulations in the light of those decisions. Cases are already being referred to the European Court of Justice from the courts of other Member States.

2 – Scope

To Whom do the Regulations Apply? [2.1]

In order to comprehend the Regulations, it is necessary to understand to whom they may apply. Employers must, therefore, examine the composition of the workforce.

Employees are certainly covered by the Regulations. However, there are additional groups of individuals who will fall within the wider definition of 'workers'. Thus, it is necessary to determine who 'workers' are.

Workers Working Outside Great Britain [2.2]

The definition of a 'worker' may be affected by where the worker is geographically situated, as *Regulation 1(2)* applies the Regulations to Great Britain only (see further 4.9).

The Regulations apply to England, Wales and Scotland. The Directive has been implemented separately in Northern Ireland.

It is not clear to what extent the Regulations apply to international workers. In contrast to other employment legislation, the Regulations are silent on the implications of the situation where the worker is carrying out his/her duties.

Other UK employment legislation, such as *section 196, ERA 1996*, incorporates the concept of 'ordinarily works outside Great Britain' to determine the scope of the relevant legislation. The absence of this term creates ambiguity within the Regulations. It is not clear whether an individual who is employed by a British company but spends all his/her time working abroad will be covered by the Regulations.

Whilst it is uncertain whether these workers may bring claims on the basis that they have not been allowed to exercise any rights under *Regulation 30*, they are nevertheless prevented from bringing a claim for unfair dismissal and/or detriment as these claims arise out of the *ERA 1996*.

Further, the position of the Health and Safety Executive is questionable in respect of workers overseas (see 7.2).

In practice, it is best to check what rights and obligations exist on a local basis within the foreign country in question. For example, if the individual is working in France, he/she may be covered by the French equivalent of the Regulations. It may be that local laws provide the individual with greater rights than he/she would benefit from under UK law.

Scope of the Directive [2.3]

Article 1 of the Directive states that the Directive shall apply to all sectors of activity, both public and private, within the meaning of *Article 2* of the *Framework Directive* with certain exceptions (see 3.2 below).

Article 2 of the *Framework Directive* provides as follows.

> **'Scope**
> 1. This Directive shall apply to all sectors of activity, both public and private (industrial, agricultural, commercial, administrative, service, educational, cultural, leisure, etc).
> 2. This Directive shall not be applicable where characteristics peculiar to certain specific service activities, such as the armed forces or the police, or to certain specific activities in the civil protection services inevitably conflict with it.
> In that event, the safety and health of workers must be ensured as far as possible in the light of the objectives of this Directive.'

Whilst the Directive talks of 'workers' but offers no definition of this term, the *Framework Directive* gives the following definition.

> 'Any person employed by an employer, including trainees and apprentices by excluding domestic servants.'

It is left to the domestic law of each Member State to determine who is a 'worker'.

This follows the typical approach of the EU, which does not attempt to reconcile the various definitions of 'worker' adopted by each Member State.

Scope of the Regulations [2.4]

Whilst the Directive offers no definition of the term 'worker', *Regulation 2(1)* provides a definition for the purposes of the Regulations. The Regulations state that a 'worker' means:

> 'an individual who has entered into or works under (or, where the employment has ceased, worked under) –
> (a) a contract of employment; or
> (b) any other contract whether express or implied and (if it is express) whether oral or in writing, whereby the individual undertakes to do or perform personally any work or services for another party to the contract whose status is not by virtue of the contract that of a client or customer of any profession or business undertaking carried on by the individual'.

This definition can also be found in *section 230(3), ERA 1996*. Its origins can be traced to the definition of worker contained in *Part IX* of the *Industrial Relations Act 1971*.

'Employees' [2.5]

The first part of this definition clearly means 'employees', although there is no concise meaning of this term.

There are two good ways to determine whether or not an individual is an employee.

O   Firstly, if it is shown that an individual's status fits the narrower definition of an 'employee', it will definitely fit the wider definition of 'worker'.
O   Further, whether an individual is an employee or not will affect what remedies are available (see 7.14–29).

Case law has helped to define the meaning of 'employee'. This has distinguished between the contract of service of an employee and the contract for services of a self-employed person.

Various tests have evolved over the years and numerous factors have been identified to assist in determining the status of an employee.

The 'Control' Test [2.6]

The control test is based on a simplistic view of the employment relationship and was established in early case law (*Yewens v Noakes (1880) 6 QBD 530*; *Ready-Mixed Concrete (South-East) Limited v Ministry of Pensions and National Insurance* [1968] 1 All ER 433).

It focuses on the traditional master/servant relationship, typically found with domestic staff and labourers. An employee will be told what to do, when to do it and how to do it by an employer, whereas an independent contractor or self-employed individual is his/her own master and will not be under the immediate direction or control of the employer. (It is necessary here to differentiate between good working practice, safety requirements and issues of professional integrity.)

However, where individuals provide a specialist service, it is not always easy to apply the control test. For example, a hospital surgeon would never concede to a hospital committee how an operation is to be performed but that same surgeon may be an employee of the local health authority and may be told what to do in terms of administration and control of training and budgetary requirements.

The control test is not an adequate test to determine employee status in today's society of sophisticated and highly skilled workers.

The 'Integration' Test [2.7]

A more appropriate test to use may be the integration test. This test involves asking the question, 'would an outsider looking at the business regard the worker as part and parcel of the employer's business?' (*Stevenson Jordan & Harrison Limited v MacDonald and Evans* [1952] 1 TLR 101 CA). Furthermore, if the terms and conditions of the contract between the company and the individual worker were more or less the same as those between the company and its own employees, further weight is attached to the premise that the individual is integrated into the business.

Tools and Equipment [2.8]

It is usual for self-employed individuals to provide their own tools and equipment but for employers to provide tools and equipment for employees.

This test may be inappropriate within certain industries. For example, within the computer industry a computer consultant will usually work on the computer equipment of the client for whom he/she is undertaking the assignment.

There will also be other industries where the provision of major equipment is not feasible for the consultant. However, the converse is rarely true. Namely, it would be very rare for employees to provide equipment other than the most nominal, such as pens and calculators. However, it is worth recognising that there are a few notable exceptions, such as hairdressers, who will normally have their own scissors.

Mutual Obligation [2.9]

Where there is a relationship of employee and employer, it is understood that there is a mutual obligation between the employer and the employee (*Airfix Footwear Limited v Cope [1978] ICR 1210; O'Kelly v Trusthouse Forte Plc [1983] IRLR 369; Clark v Oxfordshire Health Authority [1998] IRLR 125; Carmichael v National Power Plc The Times, 2 April 1998*).

This means that there is an obligation upon the employee not only to turn up to work but to do the work given to him/her and to take any work offered.

Meanwhile, there is an obligation on an employer to pay for the work done by an employee and to continue making work available.

The 'Personal Service' Test [2.10]

A self-employed individual enters into a contract to provide a service, rather than to provide his/her services personally, other than in certain circumstances where a particular individual's skills are required. In the majority of cases, therefore, a self-employed individual would be free to send a substitute.

If the worker is required to provide personal service (i.e. carry out the work him/herself) then, unless the reason is exceptional, this is indicative of the status of employee.

The 'In Business on His/Her Own Account' Test [2.11]

A self-employed individual is responsible for the management of his/her business. He/she will typically risk his/her own capital as well as time and may make a profit or a loss on any particular assignment.

A self-employed individual will usually have to advertise for his/her services, invoice for the work done and bear his/her own costs and overheads. He/she will also typically have his/her own professional indemnity insurance and provide his/her own tools and equipment.

A self-employed person will also have financial obligations, such as the obligation to register for VAT, prepare accounts where necessary and agree any tax liabilities in respect of his/her business with the Inland Revenue.

It is usual for a self-employed person to have a variety of clients, either concurrently with the contract under consideration or one after the other.

Where one individual works exclusively for another, there is a strong presumption that he/she is an employee. This presumption is strengthened, if the contract between the two of them specifically precludes the ability of the worker to offer his/her services to other potential employers on a coterminous basis.

However, it is not unknown for an employee to have several part-time employments, nor for a self-employed person to do all his/her work for one client at a time. This is particularly true of consultants within the computer industry where a project may typically last between one and eighteen months. This may also be true for workers within the construction industry.

The 'Multiple' Test [2.12]

The multiple test moves further away from any strict type of test (*Ready-Mixed Concrete (South-East) Limited v Ministry of Pensions and National Insurance [1968] 1 All ER 433*).

The multiple test looks at all the detail of the relationship and the situation. It evaluates the overall effect of the detail gathered and reviewed.

The Terms of the Contract [2.13]

It is not necessary for a contract to be in writing to be legally binding. Indeed, the UK is unusual amongst the developed world in the degree of written contracts of employment and contracts for services which are in evidence.

An oral or implied contract can certainly be legally binding. However, there can be difficulties in proving the exact nature of oral or implied contracts. It is, therefore, to be recommended that, wherever possible, accurate written contracts of service and contracts for services are in place.

It is vitally important to ensure that all documents and practices which may interact with the contract of employment are considered in conjunction with the contract. For example:

O the employer's expense and benefits policy document;
O relocation policy;
O sickness pay scheme; and
O practices which have been established for so long as to become expected by employees, such as two extra shopping days at Christmas.

Payment [2.14]

The method of payment will often be a strong indicator of the employment status of a worker. In particular, the method of description of the payment can be indicative of employment status. For example, if the payment is described as 'salary/wages' a presumption of employment will arise, whereas if the description is 'fees' the initial presumption would be towards self-employment.

The methods of payment and benefits normally associated with employee status include:

O holiday pay;
O sick pay;
O company car;
O mobile phone; and
O inclusion in company pension scheme.

The right to enjoy such methods of payment and privileges is a strong factor in determining employment status.

It can also be important to show the difference between the level of fees earned by a self-employed worker and the salary paid to an employed worker. A self-employed contractor, for example, may be charging higher gross fees for a contract over a specified period than a similarly skilled employee would be receiving in salary.

Premises [2.15]

An employee will normally attend specific premises between certain hours (e.g. the office receptionist can only work at the office and will normally be given specified hours during which he/she is expected to be on the switchboard).

In contrast, a self-employed person may need to attend certain premises as part of his/her duties but will often have discretion to choose when and how he/she performs those duties.

A Balance of Factors [2.16]

The courts have moved away from applying rigid tests, such as the control test, exclusively. In the case of *O'Kelly v Trusthouse Forte Plc [1983] IRLR 369 CA*, the Court of Appeal stated that it was important to:

> '... consider all aspects of the relationship, no single feature being in itself decisive and each of which may vary in weight and direction and having given such balance to the factors as seems appropriate to determine ...'.

One of the leading cases is *Lee Ting Sang v Chung Chief-Keung (1) Shun Shing Construction & Engineering Co Ltd [1990] IRLR 236 PC*. In this case, the court had to determine whether an individual was an employee or self-employed independent contractor. The court recognised that there is no single test for determining the status of an individual. However, the court referred to the 'fundamental test' as being the result of asking:

> 'is the person who has these services performing them as a person in business on his/her own account?'.

In arriving at the answer to this question, the court stated that consideration should be given to the factors in each case, including the following.

○ What degree of control is exercised over the individual?
○ Does the individual provide his/her own equipment or tools?
○ Does he/she hire his/her own helpers?
○ What degree of financial risk does he/she take?
○ What degree of responsibility does he/she have for investment and management?
○ To what extent does he/she have the opportunity to profit from sound management in the performance of this task?

It is important to note that no single factor is conclusive. An employer must look at each case in the light of its own factors and the terms and conditions of the contract.

'Workers' [2.17]

The second part of the definition (above at 2.4) opens up the application of the Regulations to a much broader spectrum of individuals than 'employees' alone.

It is arguable that this second part of the definition will include:

- ❑ freelance workers;
- ❑ teleworkers;
- ❑ home workers; and
- ❑ casual workers.

As many employers will know, this is a vexed area for determining status and many of these categories of workers will include employees, as well as workers, whose category of status is borderline.

The DTI guidance states that:

> 'In general a worker will be someone to whom an employer has a duty to provide work, who controls when and how it is done, supplies the tools and other equipment and pays tax and national insurance contributions. However, these are indicators rather than exhaustive or exclusive criteria. The majority of agency workers and freelancers are likely to be workers'.

This guidance is rather unhelpful, as the indicators identified are common indicators used to identify someone who is an employee.

It is worth noting, however, that the guidance notes specify 'agency workers' and 'freelancers' as being likely to fall within the ambit of the Regulations.

Delegation [2.18]

The key factor as to whether an individual is a worker or not is whether such an individual has the right under the agreement to delegate the work to a third party or whether the individual must personally do the work.

If the worker does have the right to delegate the work to a third person, it is likely that the individual will not be covered by the Regulations.

Conditions [2.19]

The Regulations place additional conditions on determining whether an individual is a worker.

The relationship between employer and worker must not be one of a client or customer of any profession or business undertaking carried on by the individual. For example, where an individual goes as a client to see an accountant in private practice to sort out the tax returns of the business, then the accountant will not be a worker for the purposes of the Regulations.

Additionally, where an individual engages a window cleaner to clean the windows of the individual's home, then the window cleaner may not be a worker for the purposes of the Regulations.

In both the examples, the contract between the parties is that of a contract with a customer.

Self-Employed Individuals [2.20]

The guidance notes are clear that self-employed individuals are not covered by the Regulations. The guidance notes state that:

> 'The Regulations do not apply to the genuinely self-employed. Someone is self-employed if they pursue a business activity on their own account'.

Indicators of individuals who are self-employed, according to the guidance notes, include:

○ individuals likely to be paid on the basis of an invoice or similar demand for payment;
○ individuals where the relationship is one of a client or customer;
○ individuals who can decide whether or not to accept work or how to carry it out; and
○ individuals who may choose to do the same type of work for more than one employer.

The guidance notes add confusion by referring to an individual working for more than one 'employer'. This term is commonly associated with employees. The terms 'client' and 'customer' are better terms to use, as they denote a relationship conducted at arm's length.

Services Through a Company [2.21]

Some individuals choose to sell their services through the vehicle of a company. Where the limited company and the individual are one and the same, it is not clear whether the individual in question will be a worker of that limited company or may be found to be a worker of the company to whom the services are supplied. Therefore, it is sensible practice to ensure the agreement between the employer and the supplying company includes an indemnity.

The indemnity will act as an insurance policy for the employer against any claims brought by the individual under the Regulations. It will also cover such matters as the individual bringing a claim against the employer for failing to provide the individual with entitlements, such as paid annual leave.

If the individual is successful in a claim against the employer under the Regulations, then the employer can obtain recompense against the individual by relying upon the indemnity. As with any indemnity, there will be little benefit in enforcing it against a 'man of straw'.

Young Workers [2.22]

As mentioned at 1.6, the Regulations implement parts of the *Protection of Young People at Work Directive (No 94/33/EC)*.

The term 'young worker' is defined by *Regulation 2(1)* as:

> 'a worker who has attained the age of 15 but not the age of 18 and who, as respects England and Wales, is over compulsory school age… and, as respects Scotland, is over school age…'.

The guidance notes provide further assistance by stating:

> 'In England and Wales a child can leave school on the last Friday in June if they are 16 or will be 16 before the start

of the next school year. In Scotland if a child is 16 between 1 March and 30 September in the final school year then they can leave school on 31 May; if a child is 16 between 1 October and the last day of February in the final school year then they can leave school on the first day of the Christmas holidays'.

The provisions of the Regulations that are different to young workers as opposed to adults are those regarding rest entitlements and health and capacities assessments and the exclusions and exceptions from these provisions (see 5.56 and 5.32 below).

Further, special provisions are made for young workers employed on ships (*Regulation 26* – see 3.20) and young workers in a situation of '*force majeure*' (*Regulation 27* – see 3.19) i.e. an occurrence or unforeseeable circumstance, beyond the control of an employer.

Agency Workers [2.23]

Whilst there is no definition of the term 'agency worker' within the Regulations, it is likely that such workers will fall within the definition of 'worker' contained in *Regulation 2(1)* (see 2.4 above).

In most cases, the worker will have either a contract of employment (i.e. is an employee) or a contract for services (i.e. is self-employed) with either the agent or the principal.

Where such a contract exists, the responsibility for the worker under the Regulations will lie with the party with whom the worker has contracted.

Special provision is made for agency workers in *Regulation 36* where no such contract exists. *Regulation 36* applies where an individual:

O   is supplied by a person ('the agent') to do work for another ('the principal') under a contract or other arrangements made between the agent and the principal;

O   is not, as respects that work, a worker, because of the absence of a worker's contract between the individual and the agent or the principal; and

O   is not a party to a contract under which he/she undertakes to do the work for another party to the contract whose status is, by virtue of the contract, that of a client or customer of any profession or business undertaking carried on by the individual.

Although it is hard to imagine where such a situation may arise, an example can be found in the case of *Construction Industry Training Board v Labour Force Ltd [1970] 3 All ER 220*. It was held that temporary workers supplied by an agency had neither contracts of employment with their supply company or clients, nor a contract for services but 'contracts of their own kind'. It is questionable whether the courts would decide this case in the same way today.

Where the situation does arise, *Regulation 36(2)* determines responsibility under the Regulations for agency workers. *Regulation 36(2)* states that:

> 'In a case where this regulation applies, the other provisions of these Regulations shall have effect as if there were a worker's contract for the doing of the work by the agency worker made between the agency worker and –
> (a) whichever of the agent and the principal is responsible for paying the agency worker in respect of the work; or
> (b) if neither the agent nor the principal is so responsible, whichever of them pays the agency worker in respect of the work,
> and as if that person were the agency worker's employer'.

The guidance notes state that:

> 'In the absence of a contract between the worker and either the agency or agency's client, the employer is deemed to be whoever is responsible for paying the worker, or, if neither is responsible, whichever of them in fact pays the worker'.

Existing case law may also be used to determine who is the employer of an agency worker. If, using existing case law, it can be established that the individual is an employee of the agency, then the agency will be responsible for that individual under the Regulations.

In the case of *McMeechan v Secretary of State for Employment [1995] ICR 444*, the Court of Appeal ruled that an individual on a particular engagement (rather than a general term of agreement, commonly referred to as 'being on the books') can have the status of 'employee'.

The Government has proposed new rules to govern the relationship between employment bureaux and the individuals who use them. The proposed changes will further strengthen the argument that agency workers will be the responsibility of agency bureaux.

In practical terms, agencies will have to review their terms and conditions of engagement to ensure customers agree to comply with the Regulations where necessary. For example, the customer will have to give a worker a 20 minutes' rest break where such worker's daily working time is more than six hours.

Trainees [2.24]

Non-employed trainees are specifically included within the Regulations.

Regulation 42 states that:

> '... a person receiving *relevant training*, otherwise than under a contract of employment, shall be regarded as a worker, and the person whose undertaking is providing the training shall be regarded as his employer' (emphasis added).

The term 'relevant training' (see further 4.10) is defined in *Regulation 2(1)* as meaning:

> '... work experience provided pursuant to a training course or programme, training for employment, or both, other than work experience or training –
> (a)   the immediate provider of which is an educational institution or a person whose main business is the provision of training; and
> (b)   which is provided on a course run by that institution or person'.

The guidance notes provide the examples of 'National Traineeships' or 'participating in the New Deal' as the types of trainee position that are covered by the Regulations.

Crown Employment [2.25]

Individuals in Crown employment are given protection under *Regulation 37(1)*.

Regulation 37(2) defines 'Crown employment' as:

> '... employment under or for the purposes of a Government

department or any officer or body exercising on behalf of the Crown functions conferred by a statutory provision'.

However, *Regulation 37(4)* limits the enforcement of the Regulations in the case of individuals in Crown employment, providing as follows.

'No act or omission by the Crown which is an offence under Regulation 29 [An employer who fails to comply with any of the relevant requirements shall be guilty of an offence ... liable ...to a fine] shall make the Crown criminally liable, but the High Court or, in Scotland, the Court of Session may, on the application of a person appearing to the Court to have an interest, declare any such act or omission unlawful.'

The reason for this is based on constitutional law, as the Queen cannot be convicted in her own courts.

Armed Forces [2.26]

Regulation 38 applies the Regulations to members of the Armed Forces in the same way as they apply to individuals in Crown Service, i.e. no offence under *Regulation 29* can make the Crown criminally liable (see 3.3).

A member of the Armed Forces can obtain a declaration from court to have an offence under *Regulation 29* declared unlawful.

The Armed Forces cover the Crown's air force, military and naval forces.

In addition, the Regulations apply to individuals employed by a territorial, auxiliary or volunteer reserve association established for the purposes of *Part XI* of the *Reserve Forces Act 1996*.

There are special provisions placed on the application of the Regulations to the Armed Forces regarding remedies (see 7.12 below) and record-keeping obligations for the 48 hour week and night work (see paragraphs 5.11 and 5.41 below).

House of Lords Staff [2.27]

Regulation 39 applies the Regulations to individuals in employment as 'a relevant member of the House of Lords staff'.

The term 'relevant member of the House of Lords staff' means:

> 'any person who is employed under a worker's contract with the Corporate Officer of the House of Lords' (*Regulation 39(3)*).

A relevant member of the House of Lords staff is not prevented by any rule of law or the law or practice of Parliament from presenting a complaint to an Employment Tribunal under *Regulation 30* (see 7.10).

House of Commons Staff [2.28]

The Regulations apply to the House of Commons staff in the same way they apply to the House of Lords staff (*Regulation 40*).

The term 'relevant member of the House of Commons staff' means any person:

O   who was appointed by the House of Commons Commission; or
O   who is a member of the Speaker's personal staff (*Regulation 40(4)*).

Police Service [2.29]

The Employment Appeal Tribunal has ruled in *Commisssioner of Police of the Metropolis v Lowrey-Nesbit EAT 952/97* that a police officer is not a 'worker' for the purposes of *section 230(3), ERA 1996*.

The definition of 'worker' in *section 230(3), ERA 1996* is the same as that found in *Regulation 2(1)*. However, *Regulation 41(1)* extends the Regulations to the police service to the extent that:

> 'the holding, otherwise than under a contract of employment, of the office of constable or an appointment as a police cadet shall be treated as employment, under a worker's contract, by the relevant officer'.

A 'relevant officer' is defined in *Regulation 41(3)* as:

> '(a) in relation to a member of a police force or a special constable or police cadet appointed for a police area, the chief officer of police (or, in Scotland, the chief constable);

(b) in relation to a person holding office under section 9(1)(b) or 55(1)(b) of the Police Act 1997 (police members of the National Criminal Intelligence Service and the National Crime Squad), the Director General of the National Criminal Intelligence Service or, as the case may be, the Director General of the National Crime Squad; and

(c) in relation to any other person holding the office of constable or an appointment as a police cadet, the person who has the direction and control of the body of constables or cadets in question'.

In addition, *Regulation 41(2)* extends the application of workforce agreements under the Regulations to:

○ persons holding the office of a constable; and
○ persons appointed as police cadets by an agreement between the relevant officer (see above) and a joint branch board.

The term 'joint branch board' is defined in *Regulation 41(3)* as meaning:

'a joint branch board constituted in accordance with Regulation 7(3) of the Police Federation Regulations 1969 or Regulation 7(3) of the Police Federation (Scotland) Regulations 1985'.

Agricultural Workers [2.30]

Agricultural workers are covered by the Regulations to the extent of entitlement and limits.

However, special provision is made in *Schedule 2* of the Regulations, regarding paid annual leave (*Regulation 43*). In effect, *Schedule 2* amends the leave entitlements within the Regulations for the leave year and dates upon which leave may be taken in accordance with the agricultural wages orders.

Workers who are partly employed in agriculture are afforded the same rights and entitlements as those workers who are fully employed in agriculture.

The Regulations define workers 'employed in agriculture' in accordance with the *Agriculture Wages Act 1948* or the *Agriculture Wages (Scotland) Act 1949* and a reference to a worker partly employed in agriculture is to a worker employed in agriculture whose employer also employs him/her for non-agricultural purposes.

The term 'agriculture' includes:

> 'dairy-farming, the production of any consumable produce which is grown for sale, or for consumption or other use for the purposes of a trade or business, or of any other undertaking (whether carried on for profit or not), and the use of land as grazing, meadow or pasture land of orchard or osier land or woodland, or for market gardens or nursery grounds' (*section 17* of the *Agriculture Wages Act 1948*).

The Regulations make a special case of exemptions for agricultural workers (see 5.61 and 5.69 below).

Employer [2.31]

Whilst it is obvious to focus on who is a 'worker', it is important not to forget to look at the employment relationship from both sides and remember who is the employer.

The *Framework Directive* defines an 'employer' as:

> 'any natural or legal person who has an employment relationship with the worker and has responsibility for the undertaking and/or establishment'.

The *Framework Directive* does not define what is meant by 'employment relationship'. However, the term 'employment' in the Regulations extends to workers, as well as employees.

The Regulations define 'employer' as meaning:

> 'in relation to a worker,... the person by whom the worker is (or, where the employment has ceased, was) employed' (*Regulation 2(1)*).

The guidance notes ask 'who is the employer?' and go on to provide the following answer.

> ' In general, a worker's employer will be obvious.'

The guidance notes take us no further forward in identifying who is the employer. Having stated that who is an employer will be obvious, the notes continue by talking exclusively of agency workers (see 2.23 above).

3 – Exclusions & Exceptions

Introduction [3.1]

Part III of the Regulations sets out certain sectors of activity that are excluded from the scope of the Regulations and other activities where the workers will be excepted from some of the provisions.

Exclusions [3.2]

The European Commission's original proposals for a directive extended to all economic sectors and activities. However, following negotiations between the Member States in the lead up to its implementation, the directive (as finally adopted) was stated to apply to all sectors public and private 'with the exception of air, rail, road, sea, inland waterway and lake transport, sea fishing, other work at sea and the activities of doctors in training'.

The meaning of public and private sectors is to be understood by reference to the *Framework Directive* which means that sectors such as the Armed Forces, the police and certain activities in the civil protection service are also excluded to the extent that characteristics peculiar to these sectors inevitably conflict with the principles of the *Framework Directive*.

The *Framework Directive* is the main directive implemented under *Article 118a* of the *EC Treaty* and provides for health and safety and by reference to which all other health and safety directives are enacted.

These exclusions are reflected in *Regulation 18* of the Regulations which state that the provisions do not apply (except in respect of certain entitlements of young workers):

'(a) to the following sectors of activity –
    (i)   air, rail, road, sea, inland waterway and lake transport;
    (ii) sea fishing;
    (iii) other workers at sea; or
(b) to the activities of doctors in training, or
(c) where characteristics peculiar to certain specified services
    such as the armed forces or the police, or to certain specific

activities in the civil protection services, inevitably conflict
with the provisions of these Regulations'.

Armed Forces and Civil Protection Services [3.3]

'Armed Forces' means any of the naval, military and air forces and civil
protection services, including:

○ the police;
○ the fire brigade;
○ ambulance services;
○ customs and immigration officers;
○ the prison service;
○ the coastguard;
○ lifeboat crew; and
○ other voluntary rescue services.

It should be noted that the Regulations do not provide a blanket exclusion
for the civil protection service and the Armed Forces but rather exclude
specific services and activities peculiar to them (see also 2.26).

Medical Practitioners [3.4]

Spain has referred a question to the European Court of Justice as to whether
or not certain medical practitioners would be covered by the exception
within the *Framework Directive* for certain civil protection services. This is
despite the fact that there is an implication that, as doctors in training are
specifically excluded by the Directive, doctors who have *completed* their
training are included within the scope of the Directive. Spain has asked the
question whether it is right for this implication to be drawn (*SIMAP v
Conselleria de Sanidad y Consumo de la Generalitat Valencia C-303/98*).

Young Workers [3.5]

If the employer employs young workers, even if they are directly involved
in the excluded sector, they are not excluded in respect of:

○ the obligation of the employer to provide a free health and capacities
assessment before the young worker is assigned to night work and
at regular intervals thereafter (see 5.32);

○ the entitlement to twelve hours' daily rest (see 5.46);
○ the entitlement to a rest of 48 hours in every seven days (see 5.50);
○ the entitlement to a 30 minute rest break after 4½ hours' work (see 5.56).

Employers are also not excluded from the duty to keep adequate records to show that young workers have received adequate health and capacities assessments (see 5.41).

The Future of the Exclusions [3.6]

The European Commission has stated an intention to review the exclusions from the Directive as part of its obligations to review the Directive every five years. The most recent five year period commenced on 23 November 1998. The Commission issued proposals in the *White Paper on Sectors and Activities excluded from the Working Time Directive* on 15 July 1997 to extend the provisions of the Directive to remove certain of the exclusions following discussions with specific sectors and the European employer and union representative groups.

The European Council's discussions of the Directive highlight the difficulty with the exclusions as they currently stand, which is that of knowing exactly who is covered and who is not.

In September 1998, Commissioners Padraig Flynn and Neil Kinnock issued a statement regarding the European Commission's intention to push ahead with a package of proposals as set out in the White Paper specifically to include:

○ the extension of the Directive to all non-mobile workers within the excluded sectors;
○ the extension of some general provisions of the Directive to cover mobile workers in the railway sector;
○ a proposal for a single Directive to cover the working time of all mobile workers in road transport; and
○ a proposal to adopt into EU law the agreement reached in maritime transport on seafarers' working time.

Seafarers [3.7]

The *European Agreement on the Organisation of Working Time of Seafarers* (signed in Brussels on 30 September 1998 by the Federation of Transport Workers' Unions in the European Union (EST) and the

European Community Shipowners' Association (ECSA)) sets out the maximum hours and rest periods as they have been agreed, extending to seafarers on board seagoing commercial maritime ships.

The agreement states that the limits on hours of work and rest periods will be either:

○ maximum hours of work which shall not exceed:
  - 14 hours in any 24 hour period; and
  - 72 hours in any seven day period.

OR

○ minimum hours of rest which shall not be less than:
  - 10 hours in any 24 hour period; and
  - 77 hours in any seven day period.

Hours of rest may be divided into a maximum of two periods but one of these must be at least six hours in length. The interval between the consecutive periods of rest cannot exceed 14 hours.

In addition, the agreement provides that:

○ no seafarer under the age of 18 shall work at night;
○ collective agreements may provide for exceptions;
○ records must be maintained to monitor compliance with the provisions;
○ seafarers shall possess a certificate attesting to their fitness for work;
○ seafarers shall have regular health assessments;
○ seafarers who suffer health problems due to night work shall be transferred to day work to which they are suited, wherever possible; and
○ every seafarer shall be entitled to at least four weeks' paid leave.

The agreement is based on the labour standard (ILO 180) set by the International Labour Organisation. This is only binding on Member States that have ratified the agreement. The intention has also been stated to put forward a draft council recommendation for Member States to ratify this document.

Doctors in Training [3.8]

The White Paper will also set out an intention to extend the provisions to doctors in training.

Scope of the Exclusions [3.9]

On the basis of the discussions at a European level, the exclusions are currently considered to extend to non-mobile as well as mobile workers.

In the first consultation document, the Conservative Government seemed to suggest a particularly wide scope to cover anyone whose work has clear enough connections with the sector excluded from the Directives coverage (e.g. retail staff who work in an airport). In the second consultation document, the Labour Government backed away from this position stating that there is no implication that the mere location of the work activity is significant to make workers carrying it out subject to the exclusion.

The guidance notes issued with the Regulations put the responsibility for determining who is or is not excluded onto the employer. They state that:

> 'The location of the work, for example a port, railway station, or airport, will not necessarily mean that those doing it are excluded'.

It is important to note that it is accepted in the guidance notes that the notes are not in themselves a definitive answer to the issues. The only way this issue will finally be determined is through case law.

Determining Involvement in Excluded Sector [3.10]

Confusingly, the guidance is as follows.

> 'Furthermore, neither will workers involved in the movement of goods or people to or from a mode of transport (for example, in docks or loading/unloading onto/from road vehicles) necessarily be excluded. Where workers are directly involved in the operation of the sector, such as baggage handlers, and signal maintenance staff they are more likely to be excluded from the Regulations...'

At first sight, this appears to be contradictory, as baggage handlers, who are presumably engaged in the loading or unloading of goods, appear to be at the same time excluded from and included within the Regulations.

However, the important wording here seems to be 'directly involved in the sector'. It appears that a distinction is being drawn to distinguish those who, although their duties are in some way similar, are essential rather than peripheral to the activities of the sector. For example, those who are actually loading the baggage on to the aeroplane perform an essential part in the operation of the aeroplane as it will not take off until the passengers' baggage is loaded. On this basis, they are probably excluded. However, the service would not be interrupted if people responsible for loading luggage onto a coach service to a hotel were not available. Therefore, they are probably not excluded.

This involves the employer in some fairly difficult decisions as to who is and who is not directly involved in a sector. Employers cannot assume that, simply because their business is that of road haulage, for example, all their employees are automatically excluded because the business is in an excluded sector. It is unlikely that their employees, such as those within the accounts department, will be excluded.

The position of workers whose work involves them in different activities, some of which fall within the excluded activities and some of which fall outside, is not clear.

For example, a worker who works at an airport and who normally works as a baggage handler but who, for two days a week, provides cover in the canteen, probably would not be within an excluded sector for the two days each week that he/she worked in a canteen. However, he/she would probably be within an excluded sector for the remainder of the time. It is not clear whether:

○   the worker would be treated as completely excluded; or
○   the worker would be treated as completely covered; or
○   the employer will be required to consider the rights and obligations in respect of that employee for two days a week.

The guidance notes state that there are sound reasons for maintaining that some 'own account' transport operations should be excluded from the Regulations on the basis that they fall in the road transport sector. The example given is a retail chain operating a fleet of vehicles to deliver goods to its own stores. This is on the basis that these operations are often almost identical to those undertaken by businesses operating for hire, which are clearly excluded.

This view seems to be wholly proper. However, it is slightly inconsistent with the view at European level as expressed in the European Commission's White Paper which is that own account transport workers are already covered by the Directive.

Exceptions [3.11]

Article 17 of the Directive gave Member States the option to derogate from specified Articles of the Directive in some circumstances. The UK Government has made full use of these derogations and has included them within the Regulations by way of the exceptions laid out in *Regulations 19* to *27*.

Article 17.4 states that before the expiry of a period of seven years from 23 November 1996 the Council shall, on the basis of a European Commission proposal accompanied by an appraisal report, re-examine the derogations and decide what action to take. It may be, therefore, that these provisions have limited life or may be modified.

Regulations 19 to *27* deal with categories of worker who are excepted in a variety of ways. The exception applying to each category is set out in Appendix 2.

Domestic Servants [3.12]

Domestic servants are excluded from the definition of workers under *Article 3* of the *Framework Directive* and the Government would therefore have been justified in including these in the general exclusions. However, domestic servants are excepted from only certain parts of the Regulations *(Regulation 19)*.

The provisions of the Regulations which do not apply to domestic servants are:

○ the 48 hour week *(Regulation 4(1)* and *(2)* – see 5.3);
○ the limit on average working hours for night workers *(Regulation 6(1)* and *(2)* – see 5.22);
○ the limit on maximum working hours for night workers involved in work of special hazards *(Regulation 6(7)* – see 5.27);
○ health assessment for night workers *(Regulation 7(1)* – see 5.31);
○ health and capacity assessment for young workers *(Regulation 7(2)* – see 5.31);
○ transferring a night worker to day work for health reasons *(Regulation 7(6)* – see 5.36); and
○ adequate rest breaks from monotonous or predetermined work *(Regulation 8* – see 5.45).

Domestic servants must, however, be afforded their entitlements to:

○ daily rest periods;
○ weekly rest periods;
○ rest breaks in work of more than six hours;
○ annual leave; and
○ payment for annual leave.

The common law definition of domestic servant requires the employee to sleep on the premises (*Re Junior Carlton Club* [*1992*] *1 KB 166*; *Re Keilacott and others* [*1992*] *1 KB 466*; *Re Wilkinson* [*1992*] *1 KB 584*; *Re Selfridge & Co* [*1922*] *WN 241* and *Ogle v Morgan 1 DGM*). Therefore, the definition of domestic servants is not wide enough to extend to daily cleaners and others. It remains to be seen whether the courts will be prepared to extend this definition to persons such as nannies who do not sleep on the premises.

Domestic servants have been held to include all such employees working at 'domestic establishments', which may extend to clubs (*Junior Carlton Club*, above) and certain hospitals (*Cameron v Royal London Ophthalmic Hospital* [*1940*] *4 ALL ER*). However, the Regulations limit the extent of the exception to workers employed as domestic servants 'in a private household' (*Regulation 19*).

Workers on Unmeasured Working Time [3.13]

The Regulations provide for exclusions in the case of those working on unmeasured time.

Those on unmeasured time are defined as workers engaged in activities where the special characteristics of which mean that the duration of their working time is not measured or predetermined or can be determined by the worker.

The Regulations give the following examples:

○ managing executives or other persons with autonomous decision-taking powers;
○ family workers; or
○ workers officiating at religious ceremonies in churches and religious communities.

The guidance notes indicate that the examples given are not intended to be an exhaustive list and are for illustration only.

In addition, the guidance notes state that:

'Such a situation may occur if a worker can decide when the work is to be done, or may adjust the time worked as they see fit. An indicator may be if the worker has discretion over whether to work or not on a given day without needing to consult their employer'.

It questionable how far this exception extends. For example, those who have core minimum hours but are required to work such hours as is necessary for the performance of their duties may feel that it is left to them to decide how many hours are worked. However, as these workers have discretion only in respect of the number of hours worked over and above the core hours, they are unlikely to fall within this category. As the exception applies to workers whose work is unmeasured or who set their own hours, the exceptions are unlikely to extend to those with set hours, however senior the worker may be.

In the case of workers with unmeasured time, the Regulations do not apply in respect of the:

○ 48 hour week (*Regulation 4(1)* and *(2)* – see 5.3);
○ limit on working hours for night workers *Regulation 6(1)* and *(2)* – see 5.22);
○ maximum hours of night work for those involved in work of special hazards (*Regulation 6(7)* – see 5.27);
○ entitlement to daily rest periods for adult workers (*Regulation 10(1)* – see 5.46);
○ entitlement to weekly rest periods for adult workers (*Regulation 11(1)* and *(2)* – see 5.48); and
○ entitlement to rest breaks in work of more than six hours for adult workers (*Regulation 12(1)* – see 5.52).

Those working on unmeasured time must, however, be given health assessments and, if they are night workers, afforded the right to be transferred to day work on health grounds. They must also be afforded adequate rest breaks in monotonous work and annual leave entitlements.

The exceptions in relation to the entitlement to daily and weekly rest periods and a rest break applies only to adult workers. Young workers are not excepted in respect of this.

Other Special Cases [3.14]

Regulation 21 provides for certain complex exceptions to the provisions of the Regulations for those defined as 'other special cases'. However, where the application of the Regulations is excluded by *Regulation 21* and a worker is accordingly required by his/her employer to work during a period which would otherwise bé a daily or weekly rest period or a break in work of more than six hours, then the employer must, wherever possible, allow the worker to take an equivalent period of compensatory rest.

In exceptional cases in which it is not possible, for objective reasons, for the employer to grant compensatory periods of rest, then the employer must afford the worker appropriate protection in order to safeguard the worker's health and safety.

Workers covered by the exception under *Regulation 21* for other special cases are those who:

O travel a long distance for work (see 3.15);
O are engaged in security or surveillance activities (see 3.16);
O whose activities involve the need for continuity of service or production (see 3.17);
O work in sectors where there is a foreseeable surge of activity (see 3.18); and
O workers' activities affected by exceptional circumstances (see 3.19).

If a worker falls within the definition of other special cases under *Regulation 21*, they will be excluded from the:

O limits on night work (*Regulation 6(1)* and *(2)* – see 5.22);
O limits on night work involving special hazards (*Regulation 6(7)* – see 5.27);
O entitlement to daily rest for adult workers (*Regulation 10(1)* – see 5.46);
O entitlement to weekly rest for adult workers (*Regulation 11(1)* and *(2)* – see 5.48); and
O entitlement to rest breaks in work of more than six hours (*Regulation 12(1)* – see 5.52).

This category of worker is not excluded from:

O the requirement for working time not to exceed 48 hours in a seven day period;

○   the duty of the employer to provide health assessments for night
     workers and health and capacities assessments for young workers;
○   the duty to transfer night workers to day work on health grounds;
○   the duty to provide adequate breaks in monotonous work; or
○   the annual leave provisions.

It is important to note that except in relation to *force majeure* (see 3.19)
within *Regulation 27*, the exception in relation to daily and weekly rest
periods and breaks in work of more than six hours applies only in
relation to adult workers and does not extend to young workers.

The definition of 'other special cases' covers a number of different
situations, which are set out below.

Workers Who Travel a Long Way to Work   [3.15]

Regulation 21(a) disapplies the Regulations where:

> 'the worker's activities are such that his place of work and
> place of residence are distant from one another or his different
> places of work are distant from one another'.

The guidance notes state that:

> 'This may apply to workers where, because of the distance
> from home, it is desirable for them to work longer hours
> for a short period to complete the task more quickly or
> where continual changes in the location of work make it
> impractical to set a pattern of work'.

It is not clear how this exception will apply in practice. The
Regulations require that it must be the nature of the worker's
activities which result in his/her place of work and place of residence
being distant from one another. It is, therefore, unlikely that this
will extend to workers who simply choose to live a long way from
their workplace.

It is also unclear whether the fact that the worker's activities mean that
he/she must travel a long distance to work must be a continuous state
of affairs or whether a worker required to travel around the country for
a period of three weeks but who would normally be based in one
place would be excepted from the entitlement to rest periods and rest
breaks for the duration of that three week period.

Security and Surveillance Activities [3.16]

The Regulations are also disapplied in respect of security and surveillance activities where a permanent presence is required in order to protect persons and property (*Regulation 21(b)*). Examples given within the Regulations are security guards, caretakers or security firms.

The fact that security firms have been specified in addition to security guards begs the question of whether workers who are employed by a security firm but are not themselves involved in providing the permanent presence would also be excepted under this Regulation. It is submitted, however, that this interpretation is not within the spirit of the Regulations and that the exception is only likely to extend to those directly involved in providing the security or surveillance.

Continuity of Service [3.17]

Regulation 21(c) disapplies the Regulations in situations where continuity of service or production is required. Again, the Regulations provide certain examples:

O   services relating to the reception, treatment or care provided by hospitals or similar establishments, residential institutions and prisons;
O   work at docks or airports;
O   press, radio, television, cinematographic production, postal and telecommunications services and civil protection services;
O   gas, water and electricity production, transmission and distribution, household refuse collection and incineration;
O   industries in which work cannot be interrupted on technical grounds;
O   research and development activities; and
O   agriculture.

The guidance notes indicate that this exception will apply where there is a need for round-the-clock activity. The only example given is for work that cannot be interrupted on technical grounds. It is stated that this may be the case where there is a need to keep machinery running.

As with the exclusions, it is difficult to predict exactly who will be excepted under these provisions and who will not. It is not clear whether it will be only those directly involved in the continuity of service or whether anybody in the sector or activity will be excepted. For example, in relation to the continuity of the gas supply, will the exception only apply to engineers maintaining the gas supply to households and businesses or will it also extend to workers such as those involved in issuing gas bills?

It is presumed at this stage that the exceptions are only likely to extend to those directly involved in the continuity of service but this will only finally be resolved by case law.

Surges in Activity [3.18]

Regulation 21(d) applies where there is a foreseeable surge of activity.

The examples suggested by the Regulations are:

○ agriculture;
○ tourism; and
○ postal services.

The Regulations do not attempt to expand upon this section. Again, there are difficulties with defining exactly which workers will be excluded. It is thought that the argument will again fall to be determined on how directly involved in the activity an individual is. For example, it may be appropriate to exclude a hotel manager under this Regulation but it would probably not be appropriate to exclude holiday sales representatives working in a travel agents.

'Force Majeure' [3.19]

The Regulations provide for exceptions in unusual or unforeseen circumstances by *Regulation 21(e)* and *Regulation 27* (in relation to young workers).

Regulation 21(e) disapplies the provisions of the Regulations where the worker's activities are affected by:

○ any occurrence due to unusual and unforeseen circumstances, beyond the control of the worker's employer;
○ exceptional events, the consequences of which could not have been avoided despite the exercise of all due care by the employer; or
○ an accident or the imminent risk of an accident.

Whilst the guidance notes set out that the very nature of unforeseeable circumstances makes it difficult to identify examples in advance, they suggest that the provision relates essentially to emergency situations or those that arise outside the normal course of events. They also state that the flexibility it provides is not something that could be used on a routine basis.

This means, for example, that an annual stocktake in a shop that would require employers to ask their workers to work exceptional hours for one week every year may not fall within this category. This is because it is foreseen and not an exceptional circumstance as it arises regularly. This is not beyond the control of the employer.

In addition, under *Regulation 27*, where the young worker is required to undertake work for which no adult worker is available to perform, which is of a temporary nature and is required to be performed immediately where either:

O it is occasioned by an occurrence due to an unusual and unforeseeable circumstance beyond the employer's control; or
O there are exceptional events, the consequences of which could not have been avoided despite the exercise of all due care by the employer,

the Regulations will not apply to young workers in respect of:

O the extended right to a twelve hour daily rest period (*Regulation 10(2)* – see 5.46); or
O the enhanced right to a 30 minute rest break in a working day of more than 4½ hours (*Regulation 12(4)* – see 5.56).

Where the Regulations are disapplied because of the operation of *Regulation 27* then the young worker must be afforded compensatory rest within three weeks of the occurrence.

Young Workers Employed on Ships [3.20]

Although those workers whose activities are in sea transport and other workers at sea are excluded from the provisions of the Regulations, this exclusion does not extend to young workers. *Regulation 26* disapplies the Regulations in relation to young workers whose employment is subject to Regulations under *section 55(2)(b)* of the *Merchant Shipping Act 1995* in respect of:

◯   the duty to provide health assessments before being assigned to night work (*Regulation 7(2)* – see 5.32);

◯   the twelve hour daily rest entitlement (*Regulation 10(2)* – see 5.46);

◯   the 48 hours' weekly rest (*Regulation 11(3)* – see 5.50); and

◯   the entitlement to a 30 minute rest break in work of 4½ hours or more (*Regulation 12(4)* – see 5.56).

Workers in the Armed Forces [3.21]

For a definition of workers in the Armed Forces, see 2.26 above.

Under *Regulation 25*, the requirement to keep adequate records to show that the limits have been complied with is disapplied in relation to workers serving as a member of the Armed Forces.

In relation to young workers serving as members of Armed Forces, the Regulations are also disapplied in respect of the entitlements to:

◯   a twelve hour daily rest period (*Regulation 10(2)* – see 5.46); and

◯   a 48 hour weekly rest period (*Regulation 11(3)* – see 5.50)

Where a young worker is required to work during a period which would normally be the daily or weekly rest period in accordance with this exception, he/she must be allowed an appropriate period of compensatory rest.

4 – Working Time

What is 'Working Time'? [4.1]

The concept of 'working time' underpins the rights and obligations imposed by the Regulations. It is therefore important to understand exactly what 'working time' is in order to ensure that the limits have not been exceeded.

Employers must also understand what 'working time' is in order to provide workers with their entitlement to daily and weekly rest periods. However, the definition is far from clear.

Definition of Working Time [4.2]

The definition of working time is imported into the Regulations directly from *Article 2* of the Directive and is defined as any period during which the worker is:

O   working;
O   at his/her employer's disposal; and
O   carrying out his/her activities or duties.

All three elements of the definition of working time must be satisfied for any particular time to be classified as working time. This presumably means that if an employee agrees to assist his/her employer with his/her gardening at the weekend, this would not be working time, as although the employee would be working at his/her employer's disposal, he/she would not be carrying out his/her activity or duties (unless he/she is a gardener by profession).

Working time includes:

O   any period during which the worker is receiving relevant training; and
O   any additional period that may be agreed to be working time in a relevant agreement.

The term 'work' is to be construed accordingly.

Whether or not a worker is paid is not a relevant consideration in determining whether any particular time is working time. For example, a worker may be paid for a rest break – however, if he/she is not working during this period and he/she is not carrying out his/her activity and duties, then this would not be working time. Conversely, in carrying out unpaid overtime, a worker may be working at his/her employer's disposal and carrying out his/her activities or duties. This would, therefore, be working time, even though unpaid.

In the second consultation document issued in April 1998, the Government recognised that, given the general nature of the definition of 'working time', there is scope for difference of opinion as to whether or not the definition is satisfied. It stated that, due to this, in cases of dispute, it would ultimately be for the courts to decide.

Employees 'On Call' [4.3]

In the guidance notes to the Regulations, the Government has set out its view as to working time by reference to examples. The first of these is that of a worker on call but otherwise free to pursue his/her own activities. For example, a maintenance engineer who is on call but at home gardening whilst awaiting call outs.

The view expressed is that this would not be working time as the worker is not working. However, in the example given, when the maintenance engineer answers a call, it will become working time.

It is also stated that if the worker is required to be at their place of work 'on call' but is sleeping, although he/she is available to work if necessary, the worker would not be working, so time spent asleep would not count as working time.

The case of 'on call' employees highlights the difficulty with the definition of working time. In the second consultation document, the example is given of shop assistants or waiters who may, as an inevitable aspect of their job, be waiting to serve a customer. The Government's view is that they are likely to consider themselves to be working during such a time. If this is right, then if an employee is on the employer's premises but not doing anything active, whether or not the period of inactivity is working time will be determined on the basis of the particular circumstances of each case.

A question has been referred to the European Court of Justice by

Spain as to whether or not time spent 'on call' is working time and specifically:

> '(b) where the medical practitioners concerned are on call under the contact system rather than through their actual presence at the centre, must the whole of that time be regarded as working time or only such time as is actually carrying out the activity for which they are called out...
>
> (c) where the medical practitioners concerned are on call by being present at the centre, must the whole of that time be regarded as ordinary working time or anti-social hours...' (*SIMAP v Conselleria de Sanidad y Consumo de la Generalitat Valencia C-303/98*).

The outcome of this question is awaited with interest.

Lunch Breaks [4.4]

The guidance notes indicate that a lunch break spent at leisure should not be working time. However, if a worker participates in a working lunch, this would be working time.

Travelling [4.5]

The extent of the uncertainty as to the scope of 'working time' is illustrated in the discussion of travelling time in the guidance notes, which state that:

> 'Time spent travelling to and from a place of work is unlikely to be working time as a worker would probably neither be working nor carrying out their duties'.

The use of the words 'unlikely' and 'probably' in this context show that the Government is not providing a definitive statement that travelling to and from work will not, in all circumstances, be working time. It is conceivable that an employee on a train, travelling to and from their place of work, may be reading a report, dictating or using a mobile phone to make a work-related call. He/she could, therefore, be working at his/her employer's disposal and carrying out his/her activity and duties whilst doing so. In this case, this would be working time.

The guidance notes also indicate that the worker may well be carrying out working time if he/she is engaged in travel that is required by the job. This raises the question as to whether time spent travelling for work purposes, for example, to a meeting in excess of a normal journey to and from work, would be working time.

In this respect, the cases dealing with the vicarious liability of employers for the actions of their employees may be relevant, since vicarious liability arises where employees are acting in the course of their employment. Similarly, guidance might be obtained from certain tax cases dealing with travelling time. However, although this may be relevant in determining whether the worker is at the disposal of their employer and carrying out their activity and duty, it may not determine the issue of whether or not the worker is working whilst travelling. It is hard to see how a worker asleep on a train is working even if the journey is required under his/her contract of employment.

It should also be borne in mind that, in the case of *Jones v Tower Boot Co Ltd [1997] IRLR 168*, the Court of Appeal stated that it was not appropriate to consider the common law test in a statutory context. Purposive construction requires that when considering the meaning of definitions within statute, these must be interpreted broadly with the *purpose* of the enactment in mind.

Working From Home [4.6]

A difficult area when looking at whether an activity is 'working time' is where the worker takes work home. The guidance notes state that:

> 'Where a worker took work home the time worked would only count as working time where work was performed on a basis previously agreed with the employer'.

Where there is a specific agreement between the worker and the employer as to the performance of work at home, there will be little dispute as to whether or not time spent working constitutes working time. For example, homeworkers will be carrying out working time when working from home in accordance with their contracts. Nevertheless, monitoring this may raise some issues for the employer. Compiling time sheets may help an employer to do this.

However, where a worker, who is not contractually required to work at home, takes work home with the employer's knowledge, then this would be more difficult. It is anticipated that it may be difficult for an employer to state that it is not agreed with the worker that work will be carried out at home if the employer is aware that this is a regular practice. This is particularly so if the nature of the work requires such additional time for the proper performance of the duties.

Work-Related Activities [4.7]

What is actual working time will often not be clear in practice. For example, many professionals must keep their knowledge of their particular field up-to-date by reading professional journals and items such as reports and case law. If such a worker attends work an hour early in the morning in order to spend the first hour of the day reading such professional updates, would this time count as working time? The position becomes even less clear when that worker in the first hour of the day is reading publications such as the Financial Times to ensure that he/she has the all round business awareness necessary to do his/her job.

If the reading material of the worker is directly related to his/her field of expertise, it may be felt that this is required of him/her by his/her employer to enable him/her to properly carry out his/her duties and, therefore, it may be felt that the worker is working at his/her employer's disposal and carrying out his/her activity or duties in this first hour of the day.

However, an alternative view may be taken that it is expected by the employer that the worker has the relevant knowledge to do the job and it is up to the worker to make sure that he/she acquires this knowledge in his/her own time to make him/her employable. Therefore, during this first hour of the day, the worker would not be carrying out his/her activity and duties as the employer would not consider this to be part of his/her functions. Therefore, this is not working time.

This point will have to be decided by case law.

Statutory Rights to Time Off [4.8]

It is an interesting question whether statutory time off, e.g. to pursue such things as trade union activities, will be working time. The fact that trade union representatives have a statutory right to time off may imply that the worker is not at the employer's disposal. However, as the activity could be argued to be work related, it remains to be seen how the courts will interpret this.

Working Abroad [4.9]

The Regulations are stated to extend only to Great Britain (*Regulation 1(2)*). Therefore, where the employer and the worker are both situated outside Great Britain they would not be covered by the ambit of the Regulations. However, they may fall within the scope of the Directive as implemented by another Member State (see also 2.2).

Whether time spent by workers who work abroad for part of their time will be classed as working time is not made clear by the Regulations. However, the guidance notes state that if a worker spends time working abroad, this time will count as working time for the purpose of the Regulations.

This may well be correct for workers who travel abroad for short business trips but the position is less clear for those who may, for example, be seconded overseas for short periods.

One of the requirements of the definition of working time is that the worker would be at the employer's disposal. The purpose of the trip overseas may, therefore, be relevant in this context. Presumably, if the worker has gone overseas as part of their UK duties, he/she will be at his/her employer's disposal and any time spent overseas, however long, will be working time.

However, if they are, for example, under a secondment and at the disposal of a third party then this may not be working time.

It may be prudent for employers to obligate workers working outside Great Britain to keep a record of working time.

Relevant Training [4.10]

The specific extension of working time to cover any period during which a worker is receiving relevant training was added after the second consultation period was concluded. Relevant training is defined in *Regulation 2(1)* as:

> '... work experience provided pursuant to a training course or programme, training for employment, or both, other than work experience or training –
> (a) the immediate provider of which is an educational institution or a person whose main business is the provision of training, and

(b) which is provided on a course run by that institution or person'.

If a company runs its own internal course, then any time spent on this course will be working time, as this is training for employment and is not provided by someone whose main business is the provision of training. However, the position becomes less clear in the case of a worker who is given a day release to attend an external course paid for by the employer and provided by a professional course provider.

Again, it remains to be seen how the courts will deal with this.

Relevant Agreements [4.11]

In the second consultation document, the Government states that, due to the uncertainty surrounding working time:

> 'employers may well conclude that they want to take steps to avoid such uncertainties'.

For this reason, the Regulations include the provision for employers to clarify in a relevant agreement what constitutes working time at a particular place of work.

A 'relevant agreement' (as defined in *Regulation 2(1)*) means:

O   a workforce agreement;
O   any provision of a collective agreement which forms part of a contract between the worker and his/her employer; or
O   any other agreement in writing which is legally enforceable as between the worker and his/her employer.

This provision allows employers to clarify working time either on an individual, group or whole workforce basis. The concept of relevant agreements is discussed further at 6.6.

It is important to understand that relevant agreements allow employers to clarify any 'additional period' which is to be treated as working time. An employer cannot, therefore, limit what is working time. The only flexibility, in the case of uncertainty, is to agree that any particular time is definitely working time. There is no flexibility to agree that any particular time is definitely not working time.

Records [4.12]

Record-keeping requirements are imposed upon employers under *Regulation 9* of the Regulations. The requirement is to keep records which are 'adequate to show' that the limits have been complied with. This does not necessarily mean that employers must record every hour of working time. If the records kept can demonstrate, without the need for precise calculation, that the limits will be complied with, the employer will have met its obligations.

In this respect, employers may put the onus onto the workers or managers by requiring that either workers inform their employer if they work more than a set number of hours in any particular week or by notifying managers that it is their responsibility to notify a central resource, such as the personnel department, if an individual exceeds a certain number of hours in a week. If so notified, the employer can then monitor the hours of that particular worker and either vary their pattern of work or request that the worker enter into an individual agreement to work in excess of the limits.

However, where the employer has concluded individual agreements with workers that the 48 hour limit will not apply, then a higher record-keeping requirement will be imposed in relation to working time. This requires that the employer keeps records which specify, for each such worker, the number of hours worked during each reference period in the last two years or since the agreement came into effect, if earlier. Employers should give serious consideration before inserting a standard individual agreement into contracts of employment, given the higher standard of record-keeping required.

Record-Keeping Arrangements [4.13]

Particularly where they have entered into 48 hour agreements with workers, employers should consider reviewing their record keeping arrangements. Monitoring working time may prove problematic where workers do not work standard hours, or where they carry out working time away from the workplace at the premises of customers, for example.

Employers may consider introducing a time clocking system or operating a 'sign in, sign out' procedure. Some employers already operate a time sheet system. It may be prudent for all employers to review contracts, handbooks and disciplinary procedures to ensure that the procedures put in place to monitor working time are adhered to.

5 – Rights and Obligations

Introduction [5.1]

Part II of the Regulations sets out rights granted to workers and obligations conferred upon employers concerning working time and breaks from it.

The important distinction between workers' rights and employers' obligations is that, whilst infringement of both the rights and obligations may result in claims brought by workers, the obligations are also enforceable by the Health and Safety Executive or, in certain circumstances, the Local Authority (see 7.2). Breaches of the obligations may result in criminal prosecution.

Obligations [5.2]

Regulations 4 to *8* impose certain obligations upon employers to ensure that a number of limits on working time are complied with. These are set out in detail below.

Maximum Weekly Working Time [5.3]

The most widely known of all the provisions within the Regulations is the limit on the maximum average hours that may be worked each week. British workers work some of the longest hours in Europe and many European countries have included a lower maximum into their domestic law. The UK. This is discussed in more detail at 1.5. However, the recent study on hours and holidays by IDS (*IDS Study 657*, October 1998) finds that there has been a general move towards reducing hours in the early 1990s, although this trend is now slowing down.

The extent of the impact of the limit on working hours and patterns of work remains to be seen in the light of the possible opt-out from it.

In addition to the industry sectors that are excluded from the majority of the provisions, those workers who fall within the definition of workers with unmeasured time under *Regulation 20* are excepted for the maximum average weekly working time, as are domestic servants (see 3.12).

The limit on weekly working time is derived from *Article 6* of the Directive and is reproduced in *Regulation 4(1)* under which a worker's working time shall not exceed an average of 48 hours for each seven day period. It is specifically stated that working time is to include overtime in this respect. The concept of working time is discussed in Chapter 4.

It is a misconception that this limit requires that a worker cannot work for more than 48 hours in any given week. The limit on the hours is by reference to the *average* worked within a particular period. This means that an employee is able to work in excess of 48 hours in any particular week as long as that employee's hours average out to 48 hours or less over the appropriate reference period.

It is the duty of the Health and Safety Executive or Local Authority (in certain instances) to enforce this limit (see 7.2).

Employers' Duties [5.4]

The onus is put on the employer to take all reasonable steps to ensure that the 48 hour limit is complied with in respect of each worker employed by the employer who is not excluded or excepted from this provision (*Regulation 4(2)*).

In order to comply with the limit, employers may consider either entering into individual agreements to disapply the limit in relation to that worker or to reduce the worker's hours of work (see 6.3).

The employer may also consider reducing the worker's remuneration accordingly. An employer should always remember that any such change may be a variation of contract to which the worker's consent is required. Any unilateral imposition of a variation of contract may result in a claim for breach of contract or for unlawful deduction from wages.

Reference Period [5.5]

The Directive sets out a maximum reference period for calculating the average number of hours worked of four months (*Article 16.2*) which could be adopted into National law. The Government, for simplicity, preferred that the calculation be based on whole weeks. It therefore adopted a 17 week reference period, being the closest number of complete weeks to the maximum reference period of four months set down by the Directive.

The average number of hours worked in each seven day period is calculated on the basis of a reference period. This reference period is any period of 17 weeks in the course of the worker's employment, except in the case of those workers who fall within the definition of 'other special cases' under *Regulation 21* (see 3.14). If this definition applies, then the reference period for these workers is any period of 26 weeks.

For any worker who has worked for his/her employer for less than the reference period relevant to him/her, the reference period is that period which has elapsed since he/she started work. Therefore, a worker who has worked only one week has a reference period of one week and cannot work in excess of 48 hours in that first week without his/her consent.

This provision also protects temporary workers on short term contracts of less than 17 weeks.

Amending the Reference Period   [5.6]

The employer has the option to amend the reference period to successive periods of 17 or 26 weeks as may be the case in a relevant agreement. Otherwise, it can amend the reference period to any other period up to a maximum of 52 weeks in a collective or workforce agreement, provided that this is for objective or technical reasons or reasons related to the organisation of work.

Employers who have some workers who fall within the exceptions within *Regulation 21* and some who do not will have to consider different reference periods for each of these classes of worker. These employers may wish to consider entering into a collective or workforce agreement to harmonise these reference periods. This may well constitute an objective reason for doing so.

Relevant agreements include:

O   any agreement which forms the contract or part of the contract between the employer and the worker; or
O   any other agreement in writing which is legally enforceable as between the worker and his/her employer (see further 6.6).

This means that, if successive rather than rolling reference periods are required, this may be agreed on an individual basis in addition to on a collective basis. However, an agreement to amend the reference period to a different length period may only be agreed on a collective basis.

Calculating the Average Hours Worked [5.7]

The Regulations stipulate that the formula to be applied in calculating the average hours worked in any reference period is as follows.

$$\frac{A + B}{C}$$

Where:

A = the total hours of working time in the reference period.

B = the time worked in the equivalent number of days after the end of the reference period in which the worker has worked if any excluded days have fallen within the reference period.

C = the number of weeks in the reference period.

Excluded Days [5.8]

Article 16.2 of the Directive requires that periods of annual leave granted in accordance with the Directive (see further 5.58) and periods of sick leave shall not be included or shall be neutral in the calculation of the average number of hours worked.

The Regulations, therefore, specify that, for the purpose of calculating the average hours in any reference period, certain days are excluded (*Regulation 4(7)*).

These 'excluded days' are:

- any period of statutory annual leave entitlement;
- any period of sick leave;
- any period of maternity leave; and
- any period during which an individual agreement to disapply the maximum working week in relation to the worker is in force (see below at 6.3).

This means if a worker has any time off sick or any statutory annual leave during the reference period, then the time worked in an equivalent number of the working days after the end of the period must be added to the total hours worked in the reference period.

Any time off for periods which are not 'excluded days' will not be taken into account for the purposes of the calculation. Therefore, no adjustment needs to be made for any contractual holiday entitlement in excess of the statutory entitlement to annual leave or for other days off such as paternity leave or jury service.

If the worker does not work for a number of days after the end of the reference period in which 'excluded days' have fallen, these days are ignored. It is the time worked in the first days in which the worker actually carries out some work which are taken into account.

Once an individual agreement to disapply the limit on the average weekly working time in relation to a particular worker is terminated, the employer must make an adjustment to the averaging calculation for the excluded days during which the agreement was in force.

Oddly, the Regulations in draft form limited the 'excluded days' to be taken into account to days on which the worker would normally have worked. However, this has been removed in their final form. It is not clear whether this removal means that days on which the worker would normally not have worked, such as bank holidays, are now to be treated as excluded days.

Example Calculations [5.9]

To illustrate how the calculation works in practice, the guidance notes have set out two examples. Example 1 sets out how the average is calculated if there are no 'excluded days' within that period.

Example 1

A worker has a standard working week of 40 hours and does overtime of 12 hours a week for the first 10 weeks of the 17-week reference period. No leave is taken during the reference period.

The total hours worked is:
17 weeks of 40 hours and 10 weeks of 12 hours of overtime
$(17 \times 40) + (10 \times 12) = 800$

Therefore his/her average (total hours divided by number of weeks):
$$\frac{800}{17}$$
$= 47.1$ hours a week

Therefore, the average limit of 48 hours has been complied with.

Example 2 in the guidance notes then illustrates how this calculation varies if there are any excluded days in the period.

Example 2

A worker has a standard working week of 40 hours (8 hours a day) and does overtime of 8 hours a week for the first 12 weeks of the 17 week reference period. 4 days' annual leave entitlement are also taken during the reference period.

The total number of hours worked in the reference period is:
16 weeks and 1 day (of 40 hours a week and 8 hours a day)
and 8 weeks of 12 hours of overtime
(16 x 40) + (1 x 8) + (8 x 12) = 744

To this must be added the time worked for the 4 days of his/her annual leave entitlement. In the first 4 working days after the reference period the worker does no overtime, so 4 days of 8 hours work should be added to the total:
4 x 8 = 32

Therefore his/her average is (total hours divided by number of weeks):
$$\frac{744 + 32}{17}$$
= 45.6 hours per week

And so the average limit of 48 hours has been complied with.

Employers who operate fluctuating working hour patterns may find that some workers' hours are within the limit for part of the cycle but exceed it for other parts. Therefore, employers should monitor this class of worker more closely.

Agreement to Exclude the Maximum Working Week [5.10]

Article 18 provides that Member States have the option not to apply *Article 6* (which sets the maximum working week) provided that it takes necessary measures to ensure that:

❍ employers cannot require workers to work for more than the weekly average of 48 hours without the workers' consent;
❍ no worker is subject to detriment by his/her employer because he/ she is not willing to give his/her agreement to perform such work;

O the employer keeps up-to-date records of all workers who carry out such work;

O the records are placed at the disposal of the competent authorities, who may, if they are concerned about the health and safety of the workers, prohibit or restrict the possibility of exceeding the maximum weekly working hours; and

O the employer provides competent authorities at their request with information on cases in which agreement has been given by workers to perform work exceeding 48 hours over a period of seven days.

The Government has taken up this option within *Regulation 5* of the Regulations which gives workers and employers the opportunity to agree in writing that the limit on the maximum average weekly hours which may be worked in a seven day period will not apply to that worker.

However, *Article 18* of the Directive also states that before the expiry of a period of seven years from 23 November 1993, the European Council shall, on the basis of a Commission proposal accompanied by an appraisal report, re-examine the provisions of this point and decide what action to take. It may be, therefore, that in time the ability to agree to work in excess of 48 hours may be removed. The European Commission has already indicated that it would prefer the Article to be removed.

Should a worker agree with the employer that the limit on the average hours of working time in each seven day period shall not apply to them, they can do so, providing this agreement is in writing. This does not require the agreement to be in the form of a contract or other legally binding document, although should the employer so wish, this could be used.

It is not possible for employers to disapply the maximum average working week in a collective or workforce agreement. Therefore, even if employers have concluded such an agreement they should, in practice, normally enter into separate individual agreements in relation to the 48 hour limit.

Record-Keeping Requirements [5.11]

Any agreement to exclude the 48 hour limit will only have the effect of disapplying the limit provided that the employer has complied with the stringent record-keeping requirements imposed by *Regulation 5*.

Regulation 5(4) requires that the employer maintains up-to-date records which:

O identify each of the workers who has entered into such an agreement;
O set out any terms upon which the workers have agreed that the limit should not apply; and
O specify the number of hours worked by each such worker during each reference period since the agreement came into effect (excluding any period which ended more than two years before the most recent entry in the records).

In addition, in order to be effective in disapplying the Regulations, the employer must permit any health and safety Inspector to inspect the records on request and must provide any such Inspector with whatever relevant information is requested by him/her (see further 7.2).

Blanket Agreements [5.12]

It is important to note that the record-keeping requirements in respect of working time are higher for those workers who have entered into agreements to exclude the 48 hour limit than the general duty imposed under *Regulation 9*.

The general duty requires simply that employers keep records which are adequate to show whether the limits specified in relation to working time have been complied with. This does not necessarily require the employer to record every hour of working time. However, if the employer has concluded an individual agreement with any of its workers, then it must keep a record of every single hour of working time for all those workers.

It is, therefore, recommended that employers do not enter into blanket 48 hour agreements with their workers as a whole, unless their systems for monitoring workers' hours already provide this detail, as employers may find it administratively burdensome.

Duration of the Agreement [5.13]

Where a worker does enter into an agreement to disapply the 48 hour average working week in relation to him/her, this can last either for a specified period or it can apply indefinitely. However, a worker must be allowed to withdraw their agreement to work in excess of this limit at any time.

Regulation 5(2)(b) provides that the worker shall be able to terminate such an agreement on giving his/her employer not less than seven days' notice.

It is possible for employers to modify this provision relating to notice within the terms of the written agreement to an alternative period of notice of up to three months. This is a useful provision, as it allows employers the opportunity to give themselves a longer period of time over which to amend or alter patterns of work should a worker decide that they no longer wish to work in excess of 48 hours.

Limits on Hours [5.14]

If workers agree that *Regulation 4(1)* shall not apply to them in respect of the maximum working week, there is then no limit set on the number of hours they may work per week, subject to any provision in the contract of employment. However, if a worker is given all his/her entitlements to daily and weekly rest periods, then he/she may not work more than 78 hours per week.

A worker may have agreed to modify or exclude the entitlements to daily and weekly rest periods and therefore, subject to his/her right to compensatory rest for the daily and weekly entitlements forgone, may work unlimited hours.

Employers should not forget that, regardless of the Regulations, they have a general duty to take all reasonable care for their workers' safety and well being which may be breached as a result of requiring a worker to work intolerable hours (*Johnstone v Bloomsbury Health Authority [1991] IRLR 118 CA*). They also have general duties to provide a safe system of work under existing health and safety legislation (*sections 2(1)* and *2(2)*, *HASAWA 1974* – see 1.3).

Pressure to Enter Agreements [5.15]

Employers who pressure their workers into signing 48 hour agreements will be opening themselves up to claims in the Employment Tribunal by the worker, as *Regulation 31* extends the *Employment Rights Act 1996* to provide workers with a right not to be subject to any detriment on the grounds of the worker's refusal or failure to sign or enter into a 48 hour agreement.

To assist in understanding the meaning of detriment, the guidance notes provide as follows.

> 'Detriment may cover a wide range of discriminatory actions, such as denial of promotion, facilities or training opportunities which the employer would otherwise have offered or made available. A reduction in pay commensurate with a reduction in working time is not necessarily a detriment, but an excessive reduction in remuneration consequent upon a reduction in working time may be.'

If a worker is an employee and is dismissed by reason of his/her failure to enter into such an agreement, then the employee who has been dismissed will be able to bring a claim for unfair dismissal. (Enforcement of the Regulations generally is discussed further at Chapter 7.)

Workers who are not employees (under the definition in *section 230(1), ERA 1996*) who are dismissed for refusing to sign such an agreement may also bring a claim but only on the basis that they have suffered detriment. Nevertheless, such a claim is limited to the same amounts that could have been claimed had the worker been an employee bringing a claim for unfair dismissal.

Work for Other Employers [5.16]

It is by no means clear that employers must take into account work that employees may carry out for other employers when considering whether the limit on the maximum weekly average hours has been exceeded.

The guidance notes state that, as part of the employer's requirement to take all reasonable steps to ensure that workers do not exceed an average of 48 hours of weekly working time, the employer is required to enquire whether the worker was working elsewhere (or request that they be notified on a worker obtaining other work). If an employer is made aware that the worker is working elsewhere, the guidance notes recommend that the employer adjusts the working arrangements accordingly or request that the worker enters into an agreement to disapply the limit on the weekly working time.

This may be burdensome for employers of workers such as part-time workers who may have a number of jobs and, for the reasons stated above at 5.12 in relation to record-keeping requirements, it may not be appropriate for employers to enter into blanket 48 hour agreements, as suggested by the guidance notes.

It is by no means clear that the Regulations themselves support the DTI's position set out in the guidance notes that employers are required to take into account working time for other employers. *Regulation 4(2)* states that it shall be an employer's responsibility to ensure that the limit on working time is complied with in the case of each worker 'employed' by the employer.

A worker's working time is defined as any period during which he/she is at his/her employer's disposal. This definition does not seem to be wide enough to require that the employer take into account the time when he/she is at the disposal of other employers. Further support can be drawn from the fact that the Regulations specifically require that employers take into account the hours worked for other employers when determining rest breaks for young workers. There is no equivalent obligation in respect of adult workers to aggregate their total working hours (*Regulation 12(4)*).

However, it would be imprudent for employers to ignore the recommendations of the guidance notes and the commercially sensible approach would seem to be to take on board the advice and make it clear in contractual documents and otherwise that employees must have the employer's permission before they take up other employment or, at the very least, notify the employer of work for other employers.

Provisions Relating To Night Work [5.17]

Studies have shown that there are additional risks to health and safety for work carried out at night. Accordingly, the Directive includes some extra checks and balances for individuals who are night workers. These have been, in the most part, incorporated into the Regulations, although certain provisions set down in the Articles have not been specifically incorporated. These are contained within *Article 12* and require that night workers be provided health and safety protection appropriate to the nature of their work and equivalent to that of other workers. The Government's view is that these requirements have been given effect through the *Management of Health and Safety at Work Regulations 1992 (SI 1992/2051)*.

Thus, certain obligations are imposed on employers who employ night workers within the meaning of the Regulations.

Night Time [5.18]

In order to understand whether or not an employer has night workers, it is first necessary to understand the concept of 'night time'. *Regulation 2(1)* defines night work as a default period between 11.00pm and 6.00am.

Employers have the option, by relevant agreement (see 6.6), to change this definition of night time, although there is not a great deal of flexibility in how far this may be changed. Night work may be agreed to be any other period of no less than seven hours. However, those seven hours must include the period between midnight and 5.00am. This gives the employer the flexibility to move night time to start at the earliest at 10.00pm or to finish at the latest at 7.00am.

Although this does not appear to be particularly useful to employers, it should be noted that if the employer wishes to modify or exclude the provisions relating to night work in any other way, this may only be done by a collective or workforce agreement. A relevant agreement gives the employer the additional option to agree on an individual basis the meaning of night work, provided that the agreement is in a legally binding form. The importance of being able to do this on an individual basis becomes more apparent once the definition of night worker is considered (see further 5.19 below).

A 'night worker' is defined as any worker who normally works at least three hours at night (see 5.19 below). It is possible, therefore, that the flexibility to amend the definition of night time could make the difference between an employer having to make special provision for night workers or not. For example, in the absence of a relevant agreement, if an employer runs a bar which is open till 2.00am and the employer employs staff between the hours of 7.00pm and 2.00am, these workers will work three hours at night time (i.e. three hours in the period between 11.00pm and 6.00am) and will therefore be night workers. If, however, he/she agrees with those workers that night time will start at 12.00pm and end at 7.00am, then only two of the workers' hours each day will fall within night time and, therefore, the employees will not be night workers for the purposes of the Regulations.

Definition of a Night Worker [5.19]

The definition of a night worker is taken from *Article 2* of the Directive and is implemented within *Regulation 2(1)* of the Regulations. This provides that a night worker is someone who, as a normal course, works at least three hours of his/her daily working time during night time.

Employers are able to substitute this definition for an alternative definition based on the proportion of the worker's annual working time worked during night time in a collective or workforce agreement.

If the employer has not substituted a definition in a collective or workforce agreement, then the employer must decide whether a worker 'as a normal course' works at least three hours at night time. The definition set out in *Regulation 2(1)* provides that a person works as a normal course (without prejudice to the generality of that expression) if he/she works such hours on the majority of days on which he/she works.

This definition is not without problems. The first consultation document stated the Government's view that 'as a normal course' meant that:

> '… if 50% or less of the employee's working days involve "night work" the employee should not be classified as a "night worker"'.

However, the guidance notes do not seem to be in accordance with this view.

The guidance notes state that:

> 'a worker may be said to work at night "as a normal course" if they do so on a regular basis, e.g. on a rotating shift pattern that results in them working regularly during night time, as opposed to an infrequent or *ad hoc* basis. Employers and workers may wish to clarify this by collective or workforce agreements'.

This definition can potentially throw up some strange anomalies. For example, it is not uncommon for employers to operate a three shift pattern. This could, therefore, result in a worker working every third week on a shift where his/her normal hours took place at night time. On the basis of the definition in the guidance notes, the worker would be working on a regular basis on a rotating shift pattern in night work. Therefore, even though only a third of his/her time was spent at night work, he/she would be a night worker. If, however, another employer operates patterns of work according to a weekly staffing rota completed at the beginning of each week on the basis of staff availability and productivity requirements and which may be different from week to week, employees would have no particular pattern to their work as they may work any shift that they agree with their manager. A worker working on this basis may end up working approximately 40% of his/her time at night time. However this would be on an *ad hoc* basis and it is arguable that, as 60% of their time is spent carrying out day work, they are not as a normal course working at night time on the majority of days on which they work.

Therefore, on the basis of the definition in the guidance notes, although the second worker is working longer hours at night than the first worker, this is not on a regular or rotating shift pattern and that worker may not be taken to fall into the definition of night worker even though the first worker working less hours will be. There seems no rationale for treating these employees on a different basis.

Reference Period   **[5.20]**

In deciding whether the majority of a worker's time is carried out at night, there is no reference period set down by the Regulations. Therefore, it is not clear whether this would need to be calculated by reference to a weekly, monthly or annual period of work on some other basis.

Workers 'On Call' At Night   **[5.21]**

Another difficulty with the definition is that it requires an understanding of whether the worker is actually working for at least three hours of his/her daily working time during night time. Therefore, where there is a question mark over whether or not any particular part of an employee's time is working time (see 4.1–4.9) it will be difficult for an employer to assess how many hours are being worked at night time.

For example, the question has been asked of the European Court of Justice whether the 'normal' hours of work referred to in *Article 8(1)* of the Directive also include 'on call' shifts performed under the contact system or while physically present (*SIMAP v Conselleria de Sanidad y Consumo de la Generalitat Valencia C-303/98*). See further 4.3.

If the example used to illustrate working time in the guidance notes relating to workers on call is taken, the guidance given is that when an individual is on call in their own time they are not working until they are actually called. It is conceivable, therefore, that employers will only be able to assess which workers are night workers retrospectively once they can assess how many times in a period the worker was called out and for what duration on each call out. They could, therefore, already be in breach of the Regulations.

It is presumed that the DTI would suggest that employers attempt to resolve this problem in a workforce or a collective agreement either by extending the definition of working time to cover all time whether or not actually called out or modifying the definition of night worker. However, as discussed below, workforce agreements are not a simple matter for employers to conclude and may not be appropriate in all cases.

Limit on Night Work [5.22]

Regulation 6(1) incorporates the requirements of *Article 8* of the Directive and sets down the limits on a night worker's normal hours.

Under *Regulation 6(1)*, a night worker's normal hours of work are limited to an average of eight hours in every 24 hours. It is the responsibility of employers to take all reasonable steps to ensure that this limit is complied with in the case of each night worker employed by that employer (*Regulation 6(2)*).

Reference Period [5.23]

As with the calculation of the limit on the maximum average weekly working time that may be worked, the average number of hours worked is calculated by reference to any period of 17 weeks during the course of the worker's employment.

Employers have the option to amend this to successive periods of 17 weeks by using a relevant agreement.

Where a worker has worked for his/her employer for less than 17 weeks, the reference period applicable will be the period that has elapsed since he/she started work for his/her employer.

'Normal' Hours [5.24]

The limit imposed is not a maximum limit on the total hours of working time which a worker may work at night but only on his/her normal hours of work. As long as a night worker's 'normal hours' do not exceed an average of eight hours, the worker may, with overtime outside normal hours, actually work in excess of eight hours in each 24 hours. However, he/she will still be covered by the maximum average of 48 hours' weekly working time imposed by *Regulation 4(1)*.

How the normal working hours are to be ascertained is governed by *Regulation 6(6)*. This provides that a worker's normal hours are to be calculated by reference to *section 234, ERA 1996* where that section applies to the worker. However, *section 234, ERA 1996* only applies to employees. Therefore, it is questionable whether this extends to workers who are not employees.

Section 234, ERA 1996 states that where an employee (as defined in *section 230(1), ERA 1996*) is entitled to overtime pay for more than a fixed number of hours in a week or other period, there are normal hours of work in his/her case. Therefore, the normal hours of work are either the employee's contractual hours or, where the employee is entitled to a guaranteed minimum number of hours' overtime, the contractual hours plus the guaranteed minimum.

Presumably, for employees who are not paid overtime, the normal hours of work will be simply the contractual hours.

Calculating the Average for Night Work [5.25]

There is an important difference between the averaging calculation for the length of night work and for the calculation of the 48 hour weekly limit.

In the case of the 48 hour limit, the total of the worker's working time is included in the calculation. However, for the purposes of the night work average, only normal working hours for that worker are taken into account (see above at 5.7).

This seems slightly strange as the intention behind the provisions of the Directive and the Regulations appear to be to acknowledge the fact that there are greater risks to health and safety from working at night. If overtime is not to be included for this limit then the extra protection will not be achieved since, provided the worker's contractual hours are eight hours or less and the worker does not have an entitlement to a guaranteed minimum number of overtime hours, the night worker is free to work the same maximum daily hours as any other worker.

For the purposes of the Regulations, the normal working hours in each 24 hours during a reference period are determined according to the following formula.

$$\frac{A}{B - C}$$

Where

A = The number of normal working hours during a reference period.
B = The number of days during the reference period.
C = The total number of hours spent by the worker in respect of their entitlement of a weekly rest period divided by 24.

It is important to note that, unlike the calculation of the average hours worked per week, no account is to be taken of any time off for sickness, annual leave or maternity leave.

Example Calculations [5.26]

The guidance notes includes two examples which show this. These are as follows.

Example 1

A night worker normally works 4 x 12 hour shifts each week.

Therefore, the total number of hours of work for a 17 week reference period would be:

17 weeks of 4 shifts of 12 hours
17 x (4 x 12) = 816

There are 119 days in the reference period and 17 weekly rest periods of 24 hours to which the worker is entitled. Therefore, C is:

$$17 \times \frac{24}{24} = 17$$

The calculation becomes (the total of hours divided by the number of days a worker could be required to work):

$$\frac{816}{119-17}$$

This equals an average of 8 hours in each 24 hour period.

Example 2

A night worker normally works 5 days of 10 hours followed by 3 days of rest. The cycle starts at the beginning of the reference period (and so there are 15 cycles of work). The worker takes 2 weeks' leave and works 6 hours' overtime a week for 3 weeks. This does not affect the calculation of normal hours, as these factors fall outside the worker's set pattern of working time.

Therefore, the total number of normal hours of work for a 17 week reference period would be:

$$15 \text{ cycles of 5 shifts of 10 hours}$$
$$15 \times (5 \times 10) = 750$$

There are 119 days in the reference period and 17 weekly rest periods of 24 hours to which the worker is entitled.

Therefore, C is:

$$\frac{750}{119-17}$$

This results in an average of 6.7 hours and so is below the 8 hour limit.

It can be seen that this can be a complex calculation if an individual has not taken their complete entitlement to daily rest periods.

Work of Special Hazards [5.27]

If a night worker's work involves special hazards or heavy physical or mental strain, then it is the employer's duty to ensure that that night worker does not work for more than an *absolute* maximum of eight hours in any 24 hour period.

As a result of a worker's entitlement to daily rest periods, there must be a break of 16 hours between each of the eight hour night working periods.

The maximum eight hours is only imposed in any 24 hour period during which the night worker performs night work. Therefore, if such a worker works on a varied shift pattern under which he/she works certain shifts in daytime and certain shifts at night time, the eight hour maximum only applies when he/she is working the night shift.

What is 'Work Involving Special Hazards'? [5.28]

Regulation 6(8) sets out what is meant by work regarded as involving special hazards or heavy physical or mental strain. It provides that work is regarded as such if:

'(a) it is identified as such in –
   (i) a collective agreement, or
   (ii) a workforce agreement,
   which takes account of the specific effects and hazards of night work, or
(b) it is recognised in a risk assessment made by the employer under Regulation 3 of the Management of Health & Safety at Work Regulations 1992 as involving a significant risk to the health or safety of workers employed by him'.

Under *Regulation 3* of the *Management of Health and Safety at Work Regulations 1992 (SI 1992/2051)*, a general duty is imposed upon employers to make a suitable and sufficient assessment of the risk of health and safety to its employees and persons not in its employment to which they may be exposed whilst they are at work.

In the first consultation document, it is noted that neither the Directive nor the Regulations indicate that it is of any necessary relevance how much of the night worker's work involves work of special hazards or heavy physical or mental strain.

The first consultation document states that the presumption must be that, if any of a night worker's work is in that category of special hazards, the absolute limit of eight hours' work in any 24 hour period applies. They do say, however, that nothing in the Regulations constrains an employer's ability to re-organise the allocation of work, perhaps with a view to confining night work with special characteristics to particular night workers in their workforce. Employers should always have regard to contractual considerations when making such variations.

Exceptions [5.29]

In addition to those workers within the excluded sectors (see 3.2), a number of other workers are excepted from the maximum average normal hours for night workers and the maximum eight hour night for those whose work involves special hazards.

The workers who are excepted are:

○   domestic servants (*Regulation 19* – see 3.12);
○   those whose working time is unmeasured as set out in *Regulation 20* (see 3.13); and
○   those workers who fall within the definition of 'other special cases' under *Regulation 21* (see 3.14).

Reduction in Pay   [5.30]

In the first consultation document, it is stated that nothing in the Directive prevents employers making a commensurate and reasonable reduction in pay or other remuneration where a worker's working time is reduced. It, therefore, suggests that, where the legislation results in a reduction in hours, it is open to employers to decide where to reduce wages:

> 'wherever such a reduction is compatible with the contract under which an employee works'.

This last sentence highlights the difficulty for employers in either reducing hours and/or reducing pay. Although in breach of the Regulations, a night worker may have agreed as part of the terms of his/her contract, that he/she will work a normal ten hour day. His/her contractual hours are, therefore, in breach of the limits on the length of night work.

Unless the employer enters into a collective or workforce agreement to amend or exclude the provisions relating to night work, the employer must reduce the worker's hours or be in breach of the Regulations. If, however, it reduces the employee's hours without his/her consent, there may be a breach of contract.

A change of hours, resulting in a reduction in pay, unilaterally imposed on the worker by the employer is likely to be taken as a serious breach of contract, entitling the worker to treat him/herself as constructively dismissed and, should he/she wish, to bring a claim for unfair dismissal and breach of contract.

In relation to an unfair dismissal claim, in these circumstances it is anticipated that the employer would be able to rely on the fair reason for dismissal set out in *section 98(2)(d), ERA 1996* in the case of an employee who could not continue to work in the position which he/she held without contravention (either on his/her part or on that of his/her employer) of a duty or restriction imposed by, or under an enactment. Further, the employer may be able to rely upon the fair reason of dismissal set out in *section 98(1)(b), ERA 1996* of some other substantial reason of a kind to justify the dismissal. However, the employer would probably be liable for damages for breach of contract.

Health Assessments [5.31]

Slightly different duties are imposed on employers to provide health assessments for adult and young workers under *Regulation 7* of the Regulations which implements *Article 9* of the Directive and *Article 9.3* of the *Young Workers Directive*.

The general obligation imposed upon employers under *Regulation 7* is that employers must not set a worker's hours such that they will fall within the definition of 'night workers' unless the worker has undertaken a health assessment before he/she takes up such duties. The health assessment can either be carried out specifically for the purpose of taking up the assignment or can be an assessment carried out on an earlier occasion, provided that the employer has no reason to believe that the assessment is no longer valid.

The assessment must be free to the worker.

Employers must then provide the worker with a free health assessment at regular intervals at whatever duration may be appropriate in his/her case.

Young Workers [5.32]

In relation to young workers, *Regulation 7(2)* extends the obligation so that the duty to carry out a health assessment arises whenever a young worker is to be assigned to work during the period between 10.00pm and 6.00am. In addition, the assessment must cover not just the young worker's health but also his/her 'capacities' to take up the assignment.

Employers are relieved from the requirement under *Regulation 7(2)* to provide a health assessment to young workers in the case where the young worker is assigned to do work of an exceptional nature.

It is important to note that young workers excepted from most of the provisions of the Regulations by reason of being directly involved in an excluded sector (see 3.2) will not be excluded from the obligation on employers to provide a health and capacities assessment in respect of young workers.

Carrying Out the Health Assessment [5.33]

The guidance notes and the Government's consultation documents point out that the *Management of Health and Safety at Work Regulations 1992 (SI 1992/2051)* already require employers to assess the risk to the health and safety of employees and to take into account employees' capabilities as regards health and safety when entrusting tasks to them. However, the Regulations firm up those requirements.

The guidance notes state that the purpose of the health assessment is to determine whether the worker is fit to carry out the night work to which he/she has been assigned.

It appears from the guidance that the purpose of the health assessment is not only to identify those whose health absolutely rules out night work altogether but also those who are suffering from a medical condition which may be exacerbated by working at night. Examples given are:

○ diabetes, particularly where treatment with insulin injection on a strict timetable is required;
○ some heart and circulatory disorders, particularly where factors such as physical stamina are affected;
○ stomach or intestinal disorders such as ulcers and conditions where the timing of a meal is particularly important;
○ medical conditions affecting sleep;
○ some chronic chest disorders where night time symptoms may be particularly troublesome; and
○ other medical conditions requiring regular medication on a strict timetable.

It does not appear that the health assessment must be a full medical carried out by a doctor. It is stated that:

'as a minimum, employers could construct a screening questionnaire for workers to complete before beginning night work'.

Should an employer opt for this minimum standard, then the questionnaire should be compiled with the guidance of a qualified health care professional, such as a doctor or nurse, familiar with the nature of the employer's business and the issues associated with working at night.

The guidance notes provide that, as a guide, the questionnaire should:

○   explain its purpose;
○   state the nature of the work to which the individual is being assigned; and
○   ask whether the worker suffers from any medical conditions or is undergoing any medical treatment such as those listed above that might affect their fitness to work at night.

It is also recommended in the guidance notes that the screening of the questionnaire should be conducted by people trained to interpret the information. It suggests that, if there are any doubts following the screening of the questionnaires, the individual should be referred to a suitably qualified health care professional for further assessment and for an opinion as to whether the worker is fit to carry out work to which he/she has been assigned. It does not appear that the person carrying out the initial screening of the questionnaire needs to be a doctor or nurse. It may be feasible for an existing safety manager to be trained by medically qualified staff to interpret the health assessment.

The guidance notes highlight that there is no one particular way to carry out a health assessment. They might be carried out, for example, by a worker's family doctor or by the employer's own company doctor or occupational health service, or by an external provider.

Whatever method is adopted by employers, it will be prudent for them to ensure that the method used is credible. For example, the guidance notes advise that, when requesting a health assessment, employers should:

○   make it clear to health care professionals that the assessments are to be conducted within the context of the Regulations; and
○   provide an explanation for the type of night work – this should include details of the duration of the work, the shift patterns and the type of work involved.

In relation to health assessments, the answers the employer receives from the workers are only as good as the information put in. Therefore, if questionnaires are prepared by doctors without full details of the functions to be carried out and the hours of work then the questionnaire produced may not be adequate to identify the particular health considerations of those workers. Similarly, if a doctor is not given full information, then he/she will be unable to adequately assess the worker's fitness for work.

Although it is not specifically stated that a worker cannot be assigned to night work, if the health assessment reveals that the worker is suffering from a medical condition which is exacerbated by night work, it may be implied from *Regulation 7(6)* which deals with the obligation to transfer night workers to day work on health grounds, where possible (see 5.36).

Frequency of Assessment [5.34]

Employers are given no more guidance in the Regulations as to how often health assessments should be carried out, other than that they should be regular.

It is stated in the consultation document and repeated in the guidance notes that the regularity of assessments will depend very much on the age and health of the individual worker and also on the type of work to be carried out. The guidance notes imply that annual screening should be the minimum standard to be applied in this respect.

Disclosing the Results of Assessment [5.35]

Although the health assessments are subject to limits on disclosure, the person carrying out the assessment may disclose to the employer without the worker's consent (or any other person other than the worker) a simple statement to the effect that the worker is fit to take up night work or to continue to undertake it. If a more detailed statement is required, this may not be given to the employer unless the worker has given his/her consent in writing to the disclosure (*Regulation 7(5)(b)*). These provisions tie in with an employer's general obligation under the *Access to Medical Records Act 1988*.

This could lead to difficulties for the employer if, for example, it is a safety manager carrying out the assessment. The safety manager must keep the information that is obtained confidential from the rest of the organisation, unless the worker's consent is obtained for its disclosure.

Transfer of Night Workers to Day Work [5.36]

Regulation 7(6) provides that, where a registered medical practitioner has advised an employer that a worker is suffering from health problems which the practitioner considers to be connected with the fact that worker performs night work, there is an obligation upon the employer, wherever possible, to transfer the worker to day work to which they are suited.

This causes several difficulties from an employer's point of view. For an employer, the first problem is understanding the extent to which they must go to satisfy the duty. There is no absolute duty to transfer to day work but instead employers must attempt to do this 'where it is possible'. Also, there is only a duty to transfer the worker to work which the worker 'is suited'. Presumably, therefore, there is no requirement to re-train a worker to take up a day position under these Regulations. However, there may be duties on employers under other legislation such as the *Disability Discrimination Act 1995*.

Failure to Find Alternative Work [5.37]

Even where the employer can show it has given its best efforts to find an alternative position in day work for the worker and has been unable to do so, despite the fact that the employer may have satisfied its obligations under the Regulations, depending on the severity of the medical condition, it may be that, by continuing to employ that worker, the employer is rendering itself liable to a civil claim for personal injury or some other claim. In these circumstances, an employer would have little choice but to terminate the worker's employment.

If an employee claimed unfair dismissal in this circumstance, the employer is likely to be able to rely on the fair reason for dismissal contained within *section 98(1)(b), ERA 1996* of 'some other substantial reason'. Whether the employer would be able to raise a defence in relation to a worker who is not an employee and who brought a claim on the basis that they have suffered detriment is not quite clear (see 7.17).

Duty to Make Reasonable Adjustments [5.38]

It should not be forgotten that, where a worker's fitness for night work becomes affected by a disability, employers have a duty under the *DDA 1995* to make reasonable adjustments which might include changes to the worker's hours.

What is not clear is how the duty to make reasonable adjustments and the duty to transfer to day work interlink. For example, it is possible that for a worker suffering from a disability or some lesser medical condition, the employer could reduce the worker's hours during night time which would prevent the medical condition from being made worse by night work. However, all of these reduced hours may still be carried out at night time. The employer would, therefore, whilst being in compliance with his/her duties under the *DDA 1995* to make reasonable adjustment, possibly be in breach of the duty under *Regulation 7(6)* to transfer the worker to day work where possible.

It is recommended that, in these circumstances, it would be prudent for an employer to obtain a second medical assessment as soon as possible, which would show that the worker's medical condition was no longer adversely affected for a reason connected with the performance of work at night.

Young Workers [5.39]

In the case of young workers, the guidance notes recommend that to deal with the added requirement for the health assessment to cover the capacities of the young worker, then the assessment should also consider issues such as physique, maturity and experience and take into account competence to undertake the night work which has been assigned.

Agreements to Amend or Modify the Provisions [5.40]

The employer has the opportunity to amend the definition of night work as discussed above at 5.17 by a relevant agreement. It also has the ability under a collective or workforce agreement to modify or exclude the application of:

O the maximum average normal working hours in every 24 hour period;
O the reference period for this average; and
O the maximum working hours imposed on night workers involved with work of special hazards and heavy, mental or physical strain.

Relevant agreements and workforce or collective agreements are discussed further at Chapter 6.

It is important to note that this does not allow employers to modify or exclude the provision relating to the obligation to provide health assessments or the duty to transfer a worker to day work where he/she is suffering from health problems relating to performing night work.

Records [5.41]

An employer has a duty under *Regulation 9* to keep records which are adequate to show whether the limits on the average normal hours or the absolute eight hour limit have been complied with in the case of each worker.

In addition, employers must also keep records to show that the obligation to provide health assessments for adults and health and capacities assessments for young workers under *Regulation 7(1)* and *7(2)* have been complied with in relation to each worker to whom the provisions apply (see 5.31).

Records must be retained for two years from the date upon which they are made (*Regulation 9(b)*).

Article 11 of the Directive requires that Member States take all measures necessary to ensure that an employer who regularly uses night workers brings this information to the attention of the competent authorities, if they so request.

The Government stated its opinion in the second consultation document that by giving the Health and Safety Executive the equivalent powers in relation to the Regulations as they have under the *Health and Safety at Work Act 1974* that they have complied with their duties under this Article (see 7.2).

Patterns of Work [5.42]

Article 13 of the Directive provides that Member States shall take the measures necessary to ensure that:

> 'an employer who intends to organise work according to a certain pattern takes account of the general principle of adapting work to the worker, with a view, in particular, to alleviating monotonous work and work at a predetermined work-rate, depending on the type of activity, and of safety and health requirements, especially as regards breaks during working time'.

It is slightly difficult to understand from this provision the exact nature of the obligation that Member States are required to impose upon employers. This was recognised by the Government in the first consultation document.

The Government's view, as set out in its second consultation document, is that the provisions of *Article 13* do not add to a great extent to the provisions of *Article 6(2)(d)* of the *Framework Directive*. This Article provides that employers shall implement measures on the basis of a number of general principles, one of which is:

> 'adapting the work to the individual, especially as regards the design of work places, a choice of work equipment and the choice of working and production methods, with a view, in particular, to alleviating monotonous work and work at a predetermined work rate and to reducing their effect on health'.

The Government has, therefore, implemented *Article 13* within *Regulation 8* to the extent that it considers that *Article 13* differs from *Article 6(2)(d)* of the *Framework Directive*, i.e. in respect of rest breaks.

Regulation 8 provides that:

> 'where the pattern according to which an employer organises work is such as to put the health and safety of a worker employed by him at risk, in particular because the work is monotonous or the work rate is predetermined, the employer shall ensure that the worker is given adequate rest breaks'.

The extent to which the rest breaks provided for under this section differ from the entitlement to a rest break under *Regulation 12* (see 5.52) is not clear. However, it may be that this imposes similar duties to those imposed on employers under *Regulation 4* of the *Health and Safety (Display Screen Equipment) Regulations 1992 (SI 1992/2792)* which provides that:

> 'every employer shall so plan the activities of users at work in his undertaking that their daily work on display screen equipment is periodically interrupted by such breaks or changes of activity as reduce their workload at that equipment'.

The guidance notes set out that work involving uninterruptable or monotonous activities may include, for example, a single task on a continuous production line.

Oddly, although this requirement is imposed upon the employer and is enforceable by the Health and Safety Executive, there is no requirement for employers to retain records of breaks provided to workers.

Other than those workers directly involved in an excluded sector, the only other class of worker who is excepted from the provisions of *Regulation 8* are domestic servants.

Entitlements [5.43]

In addition to the obligations imposed upon employers, the Regulations grant a number of entitlements to breaks from working time for workers. These are discussed in detail below.

The entitlements are derived from *Articles 3, 4, 5* and *7* in relation to rest breaks and annual leave.

In the first consultation document the view is taken that as these Articles create 'entitlements' rather than limits that must be complied with:

> '... no fault or legal liability need arise for an employer simply because a worker refuses to take up an entitlement. The Directive does not require legislation to create a situation in which, for example, an employee could render an employer liable to legal sanction by refusing to take a rest break or a minimum period of weekly rest'.

Despite this view, employers face an evidential burden in establishing that it was the worker's own decision not to take an entitlement to a rest period or break or to annual leave. The assumption may be that if a worker is not taking such an entitlement, the only reason for it is pressure of work. If the employer organises the patterns of work so as to prevent a worker form taking a rest break (see 5.52), then it has effectively denied the worker this entitlement.

Interaction of the Entitlements [5.44]

Regulation 11(7) and *Regulation 17* deal with the interaction of the entitlements to daily and weekly rest periods, rest breaks and annual leave.

Under *Regulation 11(7)* the weekly rest period may not include any period to which the worker is entitled in respect of daily rest. This may only happen where this is justified by objective or technical reasons or reasons concerning the organisation of work.

It is very difficult to understand when an objective, technical or work organisational reason may arise such as to justify this. Clearly, the only reason that a worker would be denied a daily rest period or be asked to take it at the same time as their weekly rest period is for work organisation reasons.

In the second consultation document, the Government stated a belief that 'work organisation reasons' would always be relevant to any situation where this modification of the entitlement was, in fact, in order.

This is a slightly confusing statement and does not really assist in understanding when this might apply.

The guidance notes state that:

> 'such reasons would have to be inherent in the nature of the work or its desired purpose, rather than created merely to avoid the effect of the Regulations'.

This does not appear to take us much further forward. As the consultation documents say, it would be for the courts to decide in the case of dispute about whether such a condition applied.

Although the daily and weekly rest periods must both be taken separately, where a worker is entitled to a rest break or annual leave at the same time as they take a rest period, then the two rights may not be exercised separately. However, the worker has the right to take advantage of whichever right is in any particular respect the more favourable (*Regulation 17*).

Similarly, where a worker has an entitlement under his/her contract, he/she may not exercise his/her contractual and statutory entitlements separately but may take advantage of whichever is the more favourable (*Regulation 17*).

Rest Periods [5.45]

Regulations 10 and *11* set out workers' entitlements to daily and weekly rest periods. These entitlements are enacted both from the Directive and from the *Young Workers' Directive, Article 10* of which lays down slightly longer periods of rest required for young workers than set out in the Directive for adult workers.

Daily Rest [5.46]

Under *Regulation 10(1)*, an adult worker is entitled to a rest period of not less than eleven consecutive hours in each 24 hour period during which he/she works for his/her employer. This means that a worker can, in effect, only work a maximum thirteen hour day.

The requirement is for the eleven hour rest period to be consecutive. The only time in which this may be interrupted is in the case of activities involving periods of work that are split up over the day or of short duration (*Regulation 10(3)* and *Regulation 22(1)(c)*). The Regulations give the example of cleaning staff as persons whose work may be split up over the day.

The Government stated in its second consultation document that the consecutive period does not have to fall within a calendar day and, therefore, can straddle two calendar days. This entitlement can then always be met, if the appropriate rest period is given at the effective end of working time during a calendar day. The example given in the consultation document is that someone who works between 10.00am and 2.00pm has the required entitlement to daily rest (i.e. in effect from 2.00pm on that day to 10.00am on the following day), even though there may not be eleven consecutive hours' rest during the same calendar day.

A young worker is entitled, under *Regulation 10(2)* to a slightly longer daily rest period of twelve consecutive hours in each 24 hour period.

Shift Workers [5.47]

The entitlement of adult workers to a daily rest period does not apply in relation to shift workers when they change shift and cannot take a daily rest period between the end of one shift and the start of another (*Regulation 22(1)*).

For these purposes, shift work is defined as:

> 'any method of organising work in shifts whereby workers succeed each other at the same workstations according to a certain pattern, including a rotating pattern, and which may be continuous or discontinuous, entailing the need for workers to work at different times over a given period of days or weeks' (*Regulation 22(2)*).

A shift worker is one whose schedule is part of shift work.

Where a shift worker does not receive the daily rest period on change of shift, the employer has an obligation to allow the worker, wherever possible, an equivalent period of compensatory rest (*Regulation 24(a)*).

In exceptional cases where this is not possible for an objective reason, *Regulation 24(b)* requires that the employer provide the worker with:

> 'such protection as may be appropriate in order to safeguard the worker's health and safety'.

Weekly Rest Period [5.48]

In addition to their daily rest periods, workers are entitled to a weekly uninterrupted rest period of not less than 24 hours in each seven day period

For young workers, this period is increased to 48 hours in each seven day period.

In relation to adult workers, an employer may specify, if it so requires, that instead of a 24 hour uninterrupted rest period in each seven day period, the worker may be entitled to either:

❍ two 24 hour periods in each 14 day period; or
❍ one uninterrupted rest period of not less than 48 hours in each 14 day period.

The application of this entitlement for adult workers is disapplied in relation to workers whose work may be split up over the day, as may be the case for cleaners. This gives the employer the flexibility to organise shift patterns over a fourteen day period rather than a seven day period.

It is important to note that the worker's consent to this is not required under the Regulations. The employer can impose this change unilaterally provided there is no contractual entitlement infringed. It is recommended that, if the employer wishes to provide the rest periods by reference to fourteen days rather than seven, this is clearly stated in writing, preferably in the contractual documents of the employees, in order to avoid any dispute as to whether or not the correct entitlement has been given.

Calculating the Rest Period [5.49]

The first fourteen day period is taken to begin either on 5 October 1998 or, if the worker's employment starts after that date, at the start of the week in which the employment begins.

Regulation 11(4) provides that, in the context of weekly rest periods, the entitlement is to be calculated by reference to successive periods of seven or fourteen days. The successive periods of seven or fourteen days will either start at the beginning of each week, i.e. on midnight between Sunday and Monday (*Regulation 11(6)*) or on such other days as may be provided in a relevant agreement. Therefore, if the successive period of seven and fourteen days are to start, say, on midnight between Tuesday and Wednesday, this must be provided for either individually with the worker in a legally binding written agreement or in a collective or workforce agreement.

Young Workers [5.50]

In relation to young workers, the minimum 48 hour rest break in every seven day period may be interrupted if the activities involve periods of work that are split up over the day or are of a short duration. They may also be reduced where this can be justified by the employer for technical or organisational reasons but cannot be reduced to a period of less than 36 consecutive hours (*Regulation 11(8)*).

Shift Workers [5.51]

In the case of workers who are shift workers as defined in relation to daily rest periods above at 5.47, the entitlement of adult workers to a weekly rest period does not apply in relation to a shift worker when he/she changes shift (*Regulation 22(1)(b)*).

However, where this occurs, the employer has an obligation to allow the worker, wherever possible, an equivalent period of compensatory rest (*Regulation 24(a)*). In exceptional cases when this is not possible for an objective reason, *Regulation 24(b)* requires that the employer provide the worker with:

> 'such protection as may be appropriate in order to safeguard the worker's health and safety'.

Rest Breaks [5.52]

Although some workers had a statutory entitlement to breaks in their work before the Regulations came into force (for example, workers using display screen equipment – *Regulation 4, Health and Safety (Display Screen Equipment) Regulations 1992 (S1 1992/2792)*) there has been no blanket entitlement to a rest break from working time for all workers.

Article 4 of the Directive required that Member States take measures to ensure that where the working day is longer than six hours, every worker is entitled to a rest break. No requirements were laid down as to the duration of these breaks.

In the first consultation document, the Conservative Government took the view that five minutes was an appropriate rest break. However, following the second consultation stage, this has now been increased to 20 minutes.

Regulation 12(1) states that an adult worker who works for a daily working time of six hours or more is entitled to a rest break. The duration of this break is a minimum of 20 minutes (*Regulation 12(3)*).

For young workers, *Regulation 12(4)* provides that this entitlement is to a rest break of 30 minutes where their daily working time is more than 4½ hours.

It has been questioned whether *Regulation 12(1)* provides an entitlement to a break of 20 minutes every six hours or whether it is one break of 20 minutes for each daily session at work. It appears from the wording of *Regulation 12(1)* that it is only one period of 20 minutes in any daily working time which exceeds six hours, regardless of by how much this is exceeded.

The break to which the worker is entitled must be an uninterrupted period of 20 minutes and cannot be split up into short breaks of lesser duration.

When to Take the Break [5.53]

The Regulations do not give any guidance as to when the 20 minute break should be taken. However, the guidance notes state that the break in working time should not be taken either at the start or at the end of a working day. However, there is no justification for this position in the Regulations.

The Government's justification is set out in the first consultation document in which it states that,

> 'it is implicit in the word "break" that it cannot be taken at the start or the end, of the period of working time'.

Further, it also states:

> 'that a break, as provided for, cannot overlap with the separate and additional entitlement to "daily rest"'.

What Constitutes a 'Break'? [5.54]

It is unclear exactly what would constitute a break. However, *Regulation 12(3)* states that the worker is entitled to spend the break away from his/her workstation if he/she has one. The use of the word 'entitled' suggests the worker can leave his/her workstation if he/she chooses. The important point to note is that, if he/she chooses to remain at his/her workstation, he/she must not be carrying out his/her duties.

Collective and Workforce Agreements [5.55]

Regulation 12(2) states that a collective or workforce agreement may provide for the details of the entitlement to a rest break including:

O   its duration;
O   the terms on which it is granted; and
O   when it is to be taken.

The requirement for a rest break of 20 minutes' duration is very much a fallback position if no such agreement is concluded.

Determining When the Entitlement Arises [5.56]

In the case of young workers, in determining whether or not a young worker is entitled to a rest break, the employer must take into account any work performed by the young worker for any other employers on that day. The employer must then aggregate the number of hours worked both for him/her and for each additional employer (*Regulation 11(8)*).

The fact that this is not specifically required for adult workers begs the question whether employers must aggregate hours worked for other employers by adult workers in the same way.

Pay for Rest Breaks [5.57]

The Regulations are silent as to whether a rest break must be paid for or not and the guidance notes indicate that payment is a matter to be decided between the worker and his/her employer.

Entitlement to Annual Leave [5.58]

The annual leave provisions in the Regulations are probably the most problematic and complex to understand for employers.

The recent Income Data Service study on hours and holidays for 1998 (IDS Study 657, October 1998) highlights that although the annual leave entitlement provided for in the Regulations is already commensurate with the leave provided by most employers for full-time employees, there are a large number of part-time and temporary workers who are currently given an entitlement to annual leave below the statutory minimum imposed by the Regulations.

The annual leave provisions are set out in *Regulations 13* to *16* of the Regulations. These implement *Article 7* of the Directive which requires that every worker be entitled to annual leave of at least four weeks.

Article 18.1(b)(ii) gave Member States the option to make use of a transitional period of not more than three years from 23 November 1996. During this period, the annual leave entitlement may be reduced to three weeks. The UK chose to make use of this transitional period. Therefore, *Regulation 13(2)* provides that the period of leave to which a worker is entitled under *Regulation 13(1)* is three weeks, increasing to four weeks on 23 November 1999.

Excluded Workers [5.59]

Apart from those workers who are excluded from the Regulations by reason of their direct involvement in an excluded sector, there is no class of worker who is excepted from the entitlement to annual leave.

'Leave Years' [5.60]

Regulation 13(1) provides an entitlement to leave in respect of a 'leave year'. For any worker whose leave year straddles 23 November 1999, he/she will be entitled to three weeks' leave plus a proportion of the fourth week to the extent that the holiday year straddles 23 November 1999.

This means, for example, that, for a holiday year which starts on 1 January 1999, the worker's entitlement will be three weeks plus 39/365 days x one week which equals (as part days are to be rounded up to whole days – *Regulation 13(6)*) three weeks and one day.

The worker's leave year begins on a date that is provided for in a relevant agreement, i.e. in either a contractually binding agreement with the individual worker or in a collective or workforce agreement (see 6.8). If no such agreement has been entered into, the leave year will start either:

O on 1 October 1998 for any workers whose employment began before that date and then on each anniversary of that date thereafter; or
O for workers who start work after 1 October 1998 on the date that their employment begins and each subsequent anniversary thereafter.

It is important for employers to ensure that their holiday year is specified in workers' contracts or in a collective or workforce agreement. Otherwise they may be required to calculate different workers' entitlements on the basis of different annual leave years depending upon when the workers started work.

Agricultural Workers [5.61]

For workers employed in agriculture, their leave year shall begin on 6 April in each year or such other date as may be specified in an Agricultural Wages Order which applies to that worker (*Schedule 2, Paragraph 1(a)*).

However, it is still open to employers to enter into a relevant agreement with these workers to set a different leave year.

Pay in Lieu of Leave [5.62]

Entitlement to leave may only be taken in the leave year in respect of which it is due. Therefore, leave may not be replaced by a payment in lieu except where the worker's employment is terminated (*Regulation 13(9)*). Nor may it be carried forward into another year (*Regulation 13(9)(a)*). This also means that workers cannot choose to utilise leave entitlement for a future year in an earlier year.

This prohibition on pay in lieu of annual leave and carrying annual leave forward operates only in relation to statutory annual leave under the Regulations. Therefore, an employer may pay in lieu of, or allow a worker to carry forward, any contractual entitlement in excess of annual leave.

Bank and Public Holidays [5.63]

The guidance notes point out there is no statutory entitlement to Bank and Public holidays. They suggest, therefore, that statutory days can be used to discharge an employer's obligation for providing annual leave under the Regulations. These may account for eight days (nine in Scotland) of the annual leave entitlement.

Many employers currently provide paid leave on Bank and Public holidays as a matter of contract over and above holiday entitlement. They could not, therefore, reduce holiday entitlement in any way without being in breach of contract. However, employers may wish to consider that, as Bank and Public holidays account for eight days (nine in Scotland), if these are treated as forming part of the statutory entitlement, all but seven days of the worker's holiday entitlement will be contractual and may be carried forward. The employer may also pay the worker in lieu of his/her contractual entitlement.

New Workers [5.64]

Where a worker's employment begins part way through a leave year (this would only apply where the employer has set the leave year by a relevant agreement – see 6.6), the worker will be entitled to a proportion of his/her annual leave in relation to the leave year remaining when he/she begins employment. Therefore, for a worker who starts employment at the start of the employer's holiday year, that worker will be entitled to the full three weeks' holiday entitlement during that holiday year. If, however, the worker were to start work six months into the employer's holiday year then, in the year ending 31 December 1999, the worker would be entitled to 1½ weeks' annual leave.

Entitlement to annual leave does not arise until a worker has been continuously employed for 13 weeks (*Regulation 13(7)*). For this purpose, a worker is taken to be continuously employed if his/her relations with his/her employer have been governed by contract during the whole or part of each of these weeks (*Regulation 13(8)*).

Although it is not explicit, it seems clear that once a worker has completed thirteen weeks of employment their entitlement accrues as from the first day of their employment.

A difficult situation arises if a worker commences employment towards the end of the leave year. Let us assume that a worker commences work for an employer whose leave year runs from 1 October 1998 to 30 September 1999. The worker starts work thirteen weeks and one day before the end of the leave year. On the last day of the leave year, the worker's entitlement to annual leave will arise. The leave to which he/she will be entitled, on the basis that he/she works Monday to Friday, will be:

$$\frac{92}{365} \times 15 \text{ days} = 4 \text{ working days' leave}$$
$$\text{(rounded up to the nearest day)}$$

Unfortunately for the worker, as the entitlement to annual leave has not arisen before the last day of the leave year, no annual leave has been taken and the worker now has one day in which to take four days' leave. The entitlement to annual leave cannot be carried forward and the employer cannot pay in lieu.

Although the worker has not received his/her entitlement to annual leave in accordance with the Regulations, it appears that he/she has no remedy against the employer. This is for the reason that the basis of a claim that an entitlement has not been received is that the employer has refused to permit the worker to exercise any right under *Regulation 30(1)*. The loss of the entitlement has not arisen out of any refusal by the employer but merely by reason of events. Provided that the employer allows the worker to take the one day's leave that is available to him/her, it is difficult to see what remedy the worker has.

Entitlement to Leave – What is a Week? [5.65]

As set out above, a worker's entitlement to leave is on the basis of weeks of leave. In the draft Regulations, which formed part of the second consultation document, a week was defined as the period of seven days starting at midnight between Sunday and Monday. However, this definition has been removed following the consultation stage and a week is no longer defined within the Regulations.

In common parlance a week is regularly understood as being seven days. The guidance notes state that:

> 'a week's leave should be equivalent to the time a worker would spend in a week'.

This does not assist in clarifying the meaning of a week's leave.

The guidance notes state, in one of the examples, that for a worker working five days a week, the entitlement corresponds to fifteen days' annual leave. The DTI, therefore, seems to assume that a week's leave refers to working days and assumes all the way through the discussion of annual leave that a week's leave is five days.

The IDS study on hours and holidays in 1998 states that:

> 'it is reasonably safe to assume that full-time staff work five days a week (although in practice some people work four or even six days) and on this basis, three weeks' leave equates to 15 days' holiday'.

Therefore, whilst it may be safe for most employers to assume that a week's leave is five working days, in the case of workers who regularly work more than five days then they should ensure that their workers have three complete weeks' leave.

Part-Time Workers [5.66]

One difficulty with the guidance notes is that they do not draw a clear distinction between the entitlement to annual leave and the entitlement to be *paid* for the annual leave taken.

This raises a particular problem in understanding how the provisions apply to workers such as part-time workers. The DTI's guidance is particularly confusing on this point. It provides the following example.

Example

For a worker working five days a week, the entitlement corresponds to fifteen days' annual leave.

A part-time worker, working two days a week, would have a right to six days' paid annual leave.

> If a part-time worker's working time is set in terms of hours, then their annual leave might be expressed in terms of hours too. In the case of a worker working 24 hours a week, the leave entitlement would be 72 hours.

This implies that a worker's entitlement to annual leave is *pro rata* to the hours that they work. However, the important wording in this example is 'paid annual leave'. *Regulation 13* provides for leave which is unequivocally set out as three weeks rising to four weeks on 23 November 1999 (with adjustment for those leave years which fall partly over 23 November 1999) – see further 5.71.

There is no provision within *Regulation 13* or anywhere else in the Regulations to allow for this entitlement to be *pro rata*. That this entitlement to leave must be provided in full is confirmed by the following statement in the guidance notes.

'A week's leave should be equivalent to the time a worker would work in a week. In general this should be straightforward. However, where a worker works irregular hours, the worker would have a right to annual leave that would allow them to be away from their place of work for a week.'

Once the entitlement to payment for leave is considered, then it is easier to reconcile the DTI's guidance. The entitlement to payment in respect of annual leave is dealt with under *Regulation 16*. This is a separate entitlement and is based on a calculation of a week's pay. A worker's entitlement to *paid leave* is, in effect, *pro rata* to a worker's hours. For example, a worker who works two days per week would be entitled to be away from work for a complete week but is entitled to payment for that week on the basis of a week's pay. This would be equal to pay for two working days.

If, therefore, an employer does express the worker's entitlement to leave as suggested in the example in the guidance notes, the employer should ensure that this is expressed in terms of entitlement to *paid leave*.

As the Regulations provide that the leave to which a worker is entitled under this Regulation may be taken in instalments (*Regulation 13(9)*) then it would be prudent for employers to require that, where a worker works part-time, annual leave must be taken in complete weeks to ensure that the complete entitlement is taken. Generally, it may be prudent for employers to avoid any confusion by informing employees that one week's leave will be from Monday to Sunday inclusive.

Dates on Which Leave May be Taken [5.67]

A system for workers and employers to provide each other notice of leave to be or not to be taken is set down by *Regulation 15*.

It is open to employers to vary or exclude these provisions by a relevant agreement (i.e. a contractual agreement with an individual worker or a collective or workforce agreement – see 6.8). If no such relevant agreement is entered into, then *Regulation 15* provides that, where a worker wishes to take any leave to which he/she is entitled under *Regulation 13(1)*, he/she may do so, providing he/she gives his/her employer notice.

Giving Notice [5.68]

The notice must specify:

O   the days on which leave is to be taken; and
O   if part days are to be taken, the duration of those part days.

Any such notice must be given to the employer twice as many days in advance of the first day of the leave to be taken as the number of days which the worker is intending to take. Therefore, if a worker intends to take one week's holiday, he/she must give his/her employer two weeks' notice. Similarly, if the worker intends to take two days' holiday, he/she must give the employer four days' notice.

Should an employer receive such a notice from the worker but does not wish the worker to take leave on that date, the employer may give the worker written notice of the fact. The employer's notice must specify the number of days which may not be taken. This notice must be given an equal number of days before the leave commences to the number of days' leave which are intended to be taken. If, for example, a worker gives the employer two weeks' notice of intention to take a week's holiday, the employer must give the worker a week's notice that it does not wish the worker to take his/her annual leave at this time.

In addition to the ability to provide notice to the worker that he/she may not take leave entitlement at a particular time, the employer may also issue a notice *requiring* the worker to take leave at a particular time. Any such notice must:

○   specify the days upon which leave is to be taken; or
○   if part of a day, its duration.

The notice is to be provided to the worker at least twice as many days in advance of the leave to be taken as the number of leave days the employer requires the worker to take (i.e. four days in advance for leave of two days).

Agricultural Workers – Notice [5.69]

The provisions relating to notice are slightly amended in relation to agricultural workers as the dates on which leave is to be taken by a worker employed in agriculture are to be determined in accordance with an agricultural wages order which applies to him/her. This may, however, be varied by an employer on the basis of a relevant agreement.

Failure to Provide Entitlement [5.70]

A claim may be presented to an Employment Tribunal under *Regulation 30* on the basis that the employer has refused to permit the worker to exercise a right to annual leave. If the claim is well founded, it is open to the Employment Tribunal to exercise its discretion to make an award of compensation.

It is questionable whether, in circumstances where a worker is entitled to leave but chooses not to take it, the worker has any claim against the employer.

Although, on the face of it, the employer has not refused to allow the worker to take the entitlement, it is possible that the Employment Tribunal may find that the reason why a worker has not taken their holiday entitlement is pressure of work. It may be difficult for an employer to defend a claim on the basis that it has not refused the entitlement if work pressures imposed by the employer have prevented the worker from taking leave. It remains to be seen how tribunals will interpret this provision. It may be prudent for employers to make use of the provision allowing an employer to require a worker to take leave.

Payment for Periods of Leave [5.71]

The entitlement to annual leave and the entitlement to be paid for annual leave are separate entitlements under the Regulations.

A worker is entitled to be paid in respect of a period of annual leave to which he/she is entitled under *Regulation 13* at the rate of a week's pay in respect of each week of leave.

Determining a Week's Pay [5.72]

In determining how much a week's pay is, the employer must look to *sections 221* to *224* of the *ERA 1996*. This is with modifications for the calculation date and so that the provisions relating to the maximum amount of a week's pay are removed.

Sections 221 to *224, ERA 1996* require the employer to calculate the average rate of pay over the twelve weeks previous to the period of annual leave. For the purposes of calculating the average rate of pay for the previous twelve weeks, if, in any of the twelve weeks prior to the first day of leave, the worker receives no remuneration, this week is discounted and the employer must look at earlier weeks in which remuneration was received to make up the twelve weeks.

The calculation depends upon whether the worker has 'normal hours' of work.

If the worker works under a contract which has normal hours of work which are the same each week, a week's pay is the amount payable by the worker on a normal working week (*section 221(2), ERA 1996*).

Overtime [5.73]

Overtime is not considered as normal hours for the purposes of the calculation of a week's pay unless the worker has a contractual entitlement to a guaranteed minimum number of hours overtime. If this is the case, the core hours plus the guaranteed minimum hours overtime over and above this, are treated as normal hours of work (*section 234, ERA 1996*).

Shift Workers [5.74]

For shift workers who work on different days and at different times in the day on each week, a week's pay is to be determined in accordance with *section 222, ERA 1996* with modifications for the calculation date.

This requires the employer to calculate the total number of the worker's normal working hours during the twelve weeks immediately before the first day of the annual leave to be taken. This is then divided by twelve to find the average hours worked per week. This must then be multiplied by the worker's average rate of hourly remuneration.

Amount of Remuneration [5.75]

Remuneration is not defined by statute. However, under case law, remuneration:

○ is calculated as the gross amount of pay before deduction of tax and National Insurance (*Secretary of State for Employment v John Woodrow & Sons (Builder) Ltd [1988] IRLR 11 EAT*);
○ includes wages or salaries and expenses, to the extent that they are profit in the hand of the employee;
○ excludes benefits in kind and cash payable by someone other than the employer (*S and U Stores Ltd v Wilkes [1974] 3 All ER 401*);
○ includes bonuses and other such payments if the worker is entitled to them (*Mole Mining Ltd v Jenkins [1992] IRLR 282*).

If there are payments which do not coincide with the periods for which remuneration or other payments are calculated (for example, annual bonuses) they shall be apportioned.

Piece Workers [5.76]

There is a similar calculation for piece workers to be applied under *section 221(3), ERA 1996*. This section covers those workers whose remuneration varies with the amount of work done. For these workers, the employer must calculate the average hourly rate of remuneration over the twelve weeks prior to the start of the period of current leave and multiply that by the number of normal working hours in a week.

Workers With No Normal Hours [5.77]

For workers with no normal hours, the amount of a week's pay is the amount of the worker's average weekly remuneration in the twelve weeks prior to the first day of the period of annual leave to be taken.

Termination [5.78]

The only occasion upon which employers may pay in lieu of the holiday entitlement is on termination of an employment contract.

The payments to be made on termination are set out in *Regulation 14* which applies where:

○ a worker's employment is terminated during the course of a leave year; and
○ the worker has not taken his/her leave entitlement by the date of termination.

In the leave year of termination, the leave entitlement of a worker is proportionate to the worker's period of the leave year which has expired up to the date of termination. Therefore, if a worker leaves six months into the employer's leave year, he/she will be entitled to 1½ weeks' leave.

Where, at the date of termination, part of the worker's leave entitlement remains untaken, then the employer shall make a payment in lieu of the untaken leave entitlement.

Amount to be Paid on Termination [5.79]

The amount to be paid to the worker may be provided for in a relevant agreement, i.e. in a collective or workforce agreement, or in a legally enforceable agreement with the individual worker. Many employers have agreed in contracts of employment the payments to be made on termination. These agreements would have effect for this purpose.

Where there is no provision in a relevant agreement, the Regulations provide that payment is to be made as provided for in *Regulation 16* on the basis of a period of leave determined according to the following.

$(A \times B) - C$
Where: A = The period of leave to which the worker is entitled in a leave year. B = The proportion of the leave year which has expired before the termination date. C = The period of leave taken by the worker between the start of the leave year and the termination date.

The example given by the guidance notes to illustrate this is as follows.

Example

In the case of a worker who works five days a week (i.e. 3 x 5 days' leave during the leave year) whose employment terminated six months into the leave year (i.e. half the leave year has expired) and had taken only three days' leave. The calculation would be:

$$(15 \times 0.5) - 3 = 4.5$$

Therefore, the employer should pay the worker the equivalent of 4½ days' pay.

There are also provisions to allow the employer to require the worker to compensate the employer if he/she has taken in excess of his/her entitlement (*Regulation 14(4)*).

6 – Agreements to Modify or Exclude the Provisions

Excluding or Modifying the Limits [6.1]

Generally, any provision within an agreement which purports to exclude or limit the operation of the Regulations or to prevent a person bringing proceedings under them will be void (*Regulation 35(1)*).

However, a number of the provisions of the Regulations grant employers a fairly wide flexibility to modify or exclude certain limits and entitlements by the use of various forms of agreement.

There are four forms of agreement which may be applied to achieve this end. These are all applicable in different circumstances. The agreements are:

O individual agreements – an agreement between the worker and the employer which is in writing but which is not required to have any contractual force;
O an agreement between the employer and worker which is legally enforceable and which is in writing;
O a collective agreement; and
O a workforce agreement.

Which Agreement to Use [6.2]

The relationship between these agreements is relatively complex and employers may find that to modify or exclude a particular limit or entitlement, different forms of agreement must be applied depending upon the required result.

This is illustrated in relation to the average 48 hour weekly limit on working time (see 5.3). If an employer wishes to agree with a worker that the reference period be amended to change the reference period to successive periods rather than rolling periods of 17 weeks, this may be achieved using a relevant agreement. This can, therefore, be agreed on an individual or collective basis, provided that any individual agreement is legally enforceable.

However, if the employer wishes to amend the reference period to a period other than 17 weeks, this may only be achieved by entering into a collective or workforce agreement. Contracting with workers individually to this end is not possible.

Individual Agreements [6.3]

Individual agreements are provided for under *Regulation 5* and have effect only to the extent that the employer has complied with the requirements as to record-keeping and inspection set out in *Regulation 5(4)* (see 5.11).

The only formality between the employer and the worker regarding an individual agreement is that it must be in writing.

It is not required that this agreement be contractually enforceable between the employer and the worker and, as such, does not need to form part of the contract of the worker. However, the fact that this is not required does not mean that the employer is precluded from incorporating this agreement within a contractual document.

Individual agreements may only modify or exclude *Regulation 4(1)* in relation to the maximum average weekly working time and *Regulation 5(3)* in relation to the notice period to opt out of such agreement. No other part of the Regulations may be modified or excluded by an individual agreement which is not legally enforceable between the worker and employer.

An individual agreement may be used by an employer to agree with the worker that the provisions of *Regulation 4(1)* in relation to the maximum average of 48 hours' weekly working time will not apply to that worker.

It is important to note that this is the only method by which an employer may agree with a worker that the provisions of *Regulation 4(1)* would not apply. It is not possible for the employer to modify, or exclude, this limit in either a collective or a workforce agreement.

Therefore, employers who conclude collective or workforce agreements must still enter into individual agreements with those workers who wish to work in excess of 48 hours.

Such an agreement may apply indefinitely or for a specified period (*Regulation 5(2)(a)*).

Bringing the Agreement to an End [6.4]

Where a worker agrees with the employer that the 48 hour limit will not apply to him/her, the worker is entitled to bring that agreement to an end by giving notice to the employer.

The worker is required to give seven days' notice, which must be in writing (*Regulation 5(2)(b)*).

However, the employer may agree within the individual agreement that this period of notice be amended to a period not exceeding three months. This enables an employer to provide more time for itself in which to amend working patterns should a worker bring an agreement to an end.

Current Contracts [6.5]

A number of contracts of employment at present will include provisions such as:

> 'the worker shall work such hours as are required for the proper performance of his/her duties'.

It is questionable whether such an agreement would be sufficient to be an agreement to exclude *Regulation 4(1)* (in relation to the maximum 48 hours). If the nature of the worker's duties calls for work in excess of 48 hours, it is arguable that the worker must have understood that, in entering into such an agreement, it was implied that this meant that the limit on working hours would be exceeded.

However, it is likely to be difficult to establish that a worker signing such an agreement understood that the Regulations were to be disapplied, especially where the agreement was signed before the Regulations came into force. This may also be the case even where the worker has specifically contracted to work for a number of hours per week which are in excess of 48 hours.

It is recommended that any individual agreement should be express in its intention to disapply the provisions of *Regulation 4(1)*.

Relevant Agreements [6.6]

The Regulations use the term 'relevant agreement' throughout the text.

The term relevant agreement is defined in *Regulation 2(1)* as follows.

> 'In relation to a worker, [a relevant agreement] means a workforce agreement which applies to him, any provision of a collective agreement which forms part of a contract between him and his employer, or any other agreement in writing which is legally enforceable as between the worker and his employer.'

This covers all forms of agreement, other than an individual agreement.

Therefore, this gives the employer the option in certain circumstances to choose whether or not to agree to modify or exclude certain of the provisions, either on a collective or individual basis, as opposed to certain provisions which may only be modified or excluded in a collective basis.

An employer may enter into a relevant agreement to:

○ amend the reference period 48 hour limit on average weekly working time from any period of 17 or 26 weeks to successive periods of 17 or 26 weeks;
○ amend the definition of 'night time' to an alternate period of seven hours provided that such a period includes the period between midnight and 5.00am;
○ agree any additional period of night work which is to be treated for working time for the purposes of the Regulations;
○ amend the reference period for night work from any period of seventeen weeks to successive periods of seventeen weeks;
○ state that the seven or fourteen day reference periods for daily and weekly rest periods should start on a day of the week other than at the start of each week or (as the case may be) every other week;
○ agree the duration and terms upon which rest breaks are granted for adult workers;
○ set the leave year for the purposes of entitlement to annual leave;
○ agree the provisions for determining the dates upon which annual leave entitlement is to be taken and the method for notifying the employer of the times when leave is to be taken; and
○ agree the calculation of sums payable to and by the worker in respect of annual leave entitlement untaken or exceeded on termination.

It is important to note that it is not possible, in any form of agreement, for employers to exclude the provisions for:

O   daily and weekly rest periods for young workers;
O   rest breaks of 30 minutes in 4½ hours work for young workers;
O   annual leave entitlements of any worker; or
O   health assessments for night workers and transfer to day work.

Collective Agreements [6.7]

Collective agreements are defined under *Regulation 2(1)* as an agreement within the meaning of *section 178, TULR(C)A 1992,* the parties to which are independent trade unions within the meaning of *section 5* of that Act.

A collective agreement within *section 178, TULR(C)A 1992* is any agreement or arrangement made by or on behalf of one or more trade unions and one or more employers or employers' associations. The essential feature of this definition is the requirement of negotiation. Mere consultation or discussion may not be sufficient to satisfy the definition (*Lake & Elliott Founders & Engineers Ltd and The Association of Scientific, Technical and Managerial Staffs* (CAC Award 86/3)).

An independent trade union within the meaning of *section 5, TULR(C)A 1992* means a trade union which is:

O   not under the determination or control of an employer; or
O   not liable to interference by an employer tending towards control.

To be enforceable, collective agreements must normally be incorporated into individual contracts of employment.

Collective agreements may be used in an identical manner to workforce agreements.

Workforce Agreements [6.9]

A workforce agreement is a new concept under UK law and provides employers with a non-union way to conclude an agreement to modify or exclude a variety of provisions.

The definition of a workforce agreement provides that it is an agreement between an employer and workers employed by the employer or employee representatives in respect of which the conditions set out in *Schedule 1* to the Regulations are satisfied (*Regulation 2(1)*).

Employee Representatives [6.9]

Schedule 1 sets out a number of formalities to conclude a workforce agreement and requires that, unless an employer has 20 or less employees, the agreement must be concluded with elected employee representatives.

The framework for the election of employee representatives is similar to the approach that the Government proposes to introduce to improve the operation of existing obligations in respect of elected representatives on the transfer of an undertaking and on large scale redundancies, as set out in their recent consultation document (*Employees Information and Consultation Rights on Transfer of Undertakings and Collective Redundancies* (URN 97/988) issued by the DTI in February 1998).

The existing obligations to elect representatives on transfer of undertakings and on large scale redundancies are set down in the *Trade Union and Labour Relations (Consolidation) Act 1992* and the *Transfer of Undertakings (Protection of Employment) Regulations 1981 (SI 1981/1794)* as amended.

It should be noted that there is already existing provision for employers to consult with elected representatives of their employees on health and safety at work issues. These provisions are contained in the *Health and Safety (Consultation with Employees) Regulations 1996 (SI 1996/1513)*. At present, agreements cannot be effected with such elected representatives which would affect the terms and conditions of employment.

When to Use a Workforce Agreement [6.10]

A workforce agreement may be concluded in respect of any of the workers of an employer whose terms and conditions of employment are not provided for either wholly or in part in a collective agreement. For these workers, the employer must conclude a collective agreement.

The Government has set out its belief in the second consultation document that the facility to reach workforce agreements would not undermine established collective bargaining arrangements.

It also believes that the use of a workforce agreement may be particularly apt for small and medium sized enterprises, perhaps where there are no union members among the workforce.

Workforce and Collective Agreements [6.11]

A workforce agreement and a collective agreement can both be used in the same way. They may be used in all situations where a relevant agreement may be used and in addition may:

O set an alternative definition of night worker based on the proportion of annual working time as may be worked during night time;

O for objective or technical reasons or reasons concerning the organisation of work, modify the length of the reference period for the 48 hour limit on average working time;

O be used to modify or exclude the maximum average normal working hours for night workers and the maximum working hours for those night workers whose work involves special hazards or heavy physical or mental strain;

O set the work of a night worker which shall be regarded as involving special hazards or heavy physical or mental strain;

O for adult workers, can modify or exclude the entitlement to daily and weekly rest periods;

O for an adult worker, may modify or exclude the entitlement to a rest break in work of more than six hours or set the duration and terms; or

O agree work to be identified as involving special hazards or heavy physical or mental strain.

Formal Requirements [6.12]

The formalities for concluding a workforce agreement are contained in *Schedule 1* of the Regulations.

It will be important for employers to comply with the formalities contained in *Schedule 1*. It is possible that a workforce agreement will cover workers who do not wish to be so covered, as it will be signed by elected representatives or the majority of the workforce where the employer has 20 or fewer workers. It may, therefore, be open to attack by some workers on the grounds that it is not properly concluded.

Paragraphs 1(a) and *1(b)* of *Schedule 1* provide that:

○ a workforce agreement for the purpose of the Regulations must be in writing; and

○ the agreement must also have effect for a specified period which shall not exceed five years.

To make it clear that these provisions have been complied with, it is important for the employer to specify in the agreement its commencement date and the period over which it is to run. The agreement must, therefore, be regularly renewed – at the latest, every five years. Presumably, in order to renew it the employer must renegotiate the workforce agreement and it must be signed again by the employee representatives.

The workforce agreement can either be concluded with all of the 'relevant members of the workforce' or with 'the relevant members of the workforce who belong to a particular group' (*Paragraph 1(c)* of *Schedule 1*).

For these purposes, a relevant member of the workforce is any worker employed by a particular employer, except those workers whose terms and conditions of employment are already provided for wholly or partly in a collective agreement (*Paragraph 2* of *Schedule 1*).

A particular group of relevant members of a workforce is defined as those who undertake a particular function, work at a particular work place or belong to a particular department or unit within their employer's business (*Paragraph 2* of *Schedule 1*). Therefore, although workforce agreements can be concluded with a group, this must be on a basis of a clearly identifiable group, department or unit and cannot simply be on an *ad hoc* basis.

The guidance notes state that:

> 'where it is to apply to a group of workers, the group must share a work place, function or organisational unit within the business'.

This implies that there must be a nexus between the relevant members within that particular group.

The agreement must be signed by elected representatives of the workforce or, where the workforce agreement is to apply to a group only, to elected representatives of that group (*Paragraph 1(d)(i)* of *Schedule 1*).

If the employer employs 20 or fewer workers, on the date on which the agreement was first made available for signature, then rather than by appropriate representatives, the agreement may be signed by the majority of the workers employed by the employer (*Paragraph 1(d)(ii) of Schedule 1*).

Before the agreement is made available for signature, the employer must provide all the workers to whom it is intended to apply with a copy of the text of the agreement and such guidance as those workers might reasonably require in order to fully understand it (*Paragraph 1(e) of Schedule 1*).

What is reasonable guidance for this purpose will very much depend upon the sophistication of the workforce. If the employer has a particularly unsophisticated workforce, this may require group meetings to explain the provisions. Whereas, if the employer has a particularly sophisticated workforce, it may be sufficient to provide the worker with a copy of the agreement with a written explanation of its purpose and scope.

As long as the copy of the text and guidance is given to all the workers who are anticipated to be members of the relevant workforce on the date of signing the agreement, it does not matter that the composition of the workforce has changed since the employee representatives were elected.

A workforce agreement, once signed, will bind all members of the workforce during the currency of the agreement, including any new recruits.

Elected Representatives [6.13]

In order to be effective, a workforce agreement must be signed by elected representatives of the workforce.

The representatives must be elected according to the requirements set out in *Paragraph 3, Schedule 1* of the Regulations and can be elected either to represent the members of the workforce as a whole or to represent members of a particular group.

Number of Representatives [6.14]

Under *Paragraph 3(e), Schedule 1*, the number of representatives to be elected is to be determined by the employer. There is no guidance given in the Regulations as to the number of representatives that should be elected in this respect. The use of the word 'representatives' at least indicates that there should be more than one for this purpose.

The guidance notes state that the number of representatives:

> '... will depend on the size of the workforce or the group to be represented; it is suggested that the number be sufficiently large to be representative of the workers concerned, though not so large as to make negotiations unwieldy'.

This is not particularly helpful. Common sense dictates that employers must determine what is reasonable in relation to the number and types of workers to be represented. It is unlikely to be appropriate, for example, for two representatives to represent 1,000 people. Similarly, shop floor workers are unlikely to feel adequately represented if all the elected representatives are from the senior management group.

The second consultative document suggests that:

> '... as a matter of good practice, before making a decision about such matters, an employer would want to seek and take account of views of members of the workforce'.

Eligible Employees [6.15]

All the candidates for election must be members of the relevant workforce or of the particular group (*Paragraph 3(b) of Schedule 1*).

The elected representative must be a relevant member of that group when the agreement is signed (*Paragraph 1(d) of Schedule 1*). Therefore, if a representative is elected but leaves employment during the negotiations, that representative cannot then sign the workforce agreement after termination.

Excluding Candidates [6.16]

No worker who is eligible to be a candidate must be unreasonably excluded from standing for the election (*Paragraph 3(c) of Schedule 1*). This prevents an employer from selecting a number of workers and presenting them as the potential candidates for whom the remaining workers are entitled to vote.

How far it may be reasonable for an employer to exclude a worker from an election is uncertain. It may, for example, be appropriate for an employer to exclude a worker who has learning disabilities and is unable to fully understand the process. However, if an employer were to exclude a worker on this basis, they would have to take care to comply with of the provisions of the *DDA 1995*.

Protection of Candidates [6.17]

Protection is provided to workers who stand for election or who are elected in that they have the right not to suffer detriment. This is discussed further at 7.17.

Election for Other Purposes [6.18]

The guidance notes suggest that it is possible for elected representatives:

> 'to be elected for other purposes, for example, as a 'representative employer safety' under the Health and Safety (Consultation with Employees) Regulations 1996. However, it would have to be made clear to those voting that the representatives were being elected for both purposes'.

Voting Rights [6.19]

All relevant members of the workforce must be entitled to vote for representatives of the workforce and all members of a particular group must also be entitled to vote for representatives of that group (*Paragraph 3(d)* of *Schedule 1*).

The workers must be entitled to vote for as many candidates as there are representatives to be elected (*Paragraph 3(e)* of *Schedule 1*). The election is to be conducted so as to secure that, so far as is reasonably practicable, the voting is in secret and the votes given at the election are fairly and accurately counted (*Paragraph 3(f)* of *Schedule 1*). The guidance recommends that employers may wish to consider enlisting an independent body to verify this.

Compensatory Rest [6.20]

Where a provision of the Regulations is modified or excluded by a collective or workforce agreement under *Regulation 23(a)* and as a result a worker works through a period which would normally be a daily or weekly rest period or a rest break, then *Regulation 24* imposes duties upon the employer to wherever possible allow the worker an equivalent period of compensatory rest.

In providing compensatory rest, it is not clear whether it would be adequate for employers to extend the worker's annual leave provisions to compensate him/her for loss of a rest period.

In exceptional cases where granting an equivalent period of rest is not possible for objective reasons, *Regulation 24(b)* states that the employer shall provide the worker with:

> 'such protection as may be appropriate to safeguard the worker's health and safety'.

It is not clear what form such adequate protection may take.

7 – Enforcement, Offences and Remedies

Enforcing the Regulations [7.1]

There are principally two methods of enforcing the Regulations.

O   The first involves the powers given to the Health and Safety Executive (HSE) and the Local Authorities.
O   The second involves the remedies given to the workers and employees.

Each one of these methods will be examined below. *Part IV* of the Regulations sets out the areas of enforcement, the offences and the remedies.

O   The limits contained in the Regulations, e.g. the length of night work, and the record-keeping requirements will be enforced by the Health and Safety Executive and Local Authorities.
O   The rights and entitlements contained in the Regulations, e.g. the right to annual paid leave of three weeks, are enforceable in the Employment Tribunal by the individual worker whose right or entitlement has been breached.

The Regulations do not detract from an employer's duties under existing health and safety law. Further, the Regulations do not prevent a worker pursuing a claim in the civil courts (see 7.31 below).

Enforcement – the HSE and Local Authorities [7.2]

Regulation 28 sets out the basis for enforcing the Regulations by the Health and Safety Executive and Local Authorities. Sections of the *Health and Safety at Work Act 1974* are imported into the Regulations.

The enforcement of the limits imposed by the Regulations is divided between the Health and Safety Executive and the Local Authorities (*Health and Safety (Enforcing Authority) Regulations 1998 (SI 1998/494)*).

Regulation 28(2) states that:

> 'It shall be the duty of the Health and Safety Executive to make adequate arrangements for the enforcement of the relevant requirements except to the extent that a local authority is made responsible for their enforcement ...'.

The Health and Safety Executive is responsible, in general, for enforcing the Regulations in the following areas:

- building sites;
- hospitals;
- chemical plants;
- mines;
- factories;
- nuclear installations;
- farms;
- quarries;
- fairgrounds; and
- schools.

Regulation 28(3) states in general terms that a Local Authority will be responsible for enforcing the Regulations:

> 'Where the relevant requirements apply in relation to workers employed in premises in respect of which a local authority is responsible, under the Health and Safety (Enforcing Authority) Regulations 1989 [SI 1989/1903], for enforcing any of the relevant statutory provisions, it shall be the duty of that authority to enforce those requirements'.

Thus, the Local Authority is responsible, in general, for enforcing the Regulations in the following areas:

- catering services;
- nursery facilities;
- churches;
- offices;
- consumer services;
- retail premises;
- hotels;
- sports facilities; and
- leisure centres.

Scope of the Enforcing Powers [7.3]

Regulation 28(1) states that the Health and Safety Executive and the Local Authorities' powers extend to enforcing the following provisions of the Regulations:

- the employer's duty to take reasonable steps to ensure the average 48 hour limit is complied with (*Regulation 4(2)*);
- the employer's duty to take reasonable steps to ensure the average eight hour limit on night workers is complied with (*Regulation 6(2)*);
- the absolute limit of eight hours for night workers whose work involves special hazards, or heavy, physical or mental strain is complied with (*Regulation 6(7)*);
- the employer's duty to ensure that adult night workers receive free regular health assessments (*Regulation 7(1)*);
- the employer's duty to ensure that young night workers receive free regular health and capacities assessments (*Regulation 7(2)*);
- the duty of an employer to transfer a night worker to day work where the night worker is suffering from a health problem connected with night work (*Regulation 7(6)*) ;
- the employer's duty to provide adequate rest breaks where an employer organises his/her work in such a way as to put the health and safety of a worker at risk – in particular, where the work is monotonous or the work rate is predetermined by the employer (*Regulation 8*);
- the employer's duty to keep adequate records to show that the following duties are being complied with:
  - the 48 hour limit;
  - both of the eight hour limits on night work;
  - free health assessments for adult night workers; and
  - free health and capacities assessments for young night workers (*Regulation 9*); and
- the employer's duty to provide equivalent periods of compensatory rest where the provisions on the length of night work have been modified or excluded (*Regulation 24*).

Inspectors' Powers [7.4]

The Health and Safety Executive Inspectors and the Local Authority Officers are given specific powers where they consider an employer is in breach of those aspects of the Regulations which fall within their responsibility.

The powers granted to HSE Inspectors are also granted to Local Authority Officers and include the following:

○ at any reasonable time, to enter premises which the Inspector has reason to believe it is necessary to enter for the purpose of carrying out his/her duties;

○ make such examination and investigation as may be necessary to fulfil his/her duties. For example, an Inspector may wish to examine any workforce agreement that exists, where such agreement defines the term 'night work';

○ interview any person whom the Inspector has reasonable cause to believe is in a position to give any information relevant to any examination or investigation. Failure to give an answer may be used in evidence by the Inspector. The persons an Inspector may wish to interview include:

  • an individual who has responsibility for maintaining personnel records;
  • workers; or
  • the Human Resources Director; and

○ require production of any examination (for example, a medical check) or investigation, including any statutory books which the employer is obliged to keep. For example, records of any health assessments carried out for young workers.

An Inspector may serve an 'improvement notice' on an employer who is not fulfilling its statutory obligations under the Regulations. For example, if the employer is not retaining time-keeping records for workers who have agreed to work over 48 hours per week, an Inspector can indicate this failing to an employer and require him/her to start keeping such records.

An Inspector is also given the power to issue an employer with a 'prohibition notice'. Such a notice may be issued where an Inspector is of the opinion that an activity involves a risk of serious personal injury.

Restrictions on Inspectors' Powers [7.5]

There are restrictions placed on an Inspector, regarding the disclosure of information. The information to be disclosed must be 'relevant information'.

An Inspector does not have the right to look at anything and everything. Therefore, it is best for employers to assist the Inspector with his/her investigation but monitor the information he/she is given to ensure it is 'relevant information'.

However, to prevent a person from giving a relevant answer may lead to a criminal conviction, a fine and possible imprisonment.

Employer Offences [7.6]

It will be an offence if an employer:

O   fails to comply with an improvement notice or prohibition notice;
O   obstructs or interferes with an Inspector's investigations; or
O   provides false information.

Regulation 29(1) states that:

> 'An employer who fails to comply with any of the relevant requirements shall be guilty of an offence'.

The term 'relevant requirements' means those employer's duties which an Inspector has power to investigate, as set out in paragraph 7.3 above.

An employer who is found guilty of an offence arising out of a breach of any one of the 'relevant requirements' will be guilty of a criminal offence.

Penalties [7.7]

Where an employer is found guilty of an offence under the Regulations, it may be liable to a fine or imprisonment, depending upon the seriousness of the offence committed, as follows.

O   On conviction in the Magistrate's Court, to:
  •   a fine not exceeding level 5 on the standard scale (currently a maximum of £5,000); or
  •   for more serious offences, to imprisonment for a term not exceeding six months and/or a fine not exceeding £20,000.
O   On conviction in the Crown Court:
  •   to imprisonment for a term not exceeding two years or to a fine.

The fine of £20,000 or six months' imprisonment or both arises in the Magistrates' Court where an employer fails to act upon the requirements of a prohibition notice or improvement notice.

Further, a court may order an employer to take such steps as may be necessary to remedy any breaches.

There is scope for an employer to be given a criminal conviction for each offence committed.

Who Can be Prosecuted/Fined? [7.8]

It is open to the court's discretion to decide whether the fine is levied against the employer, e.g. the company itself, or against an individual within the organisation, such as the Human Resources Director. In the case of imprisonment, it will be an individual within the organisation who serves the sentence.

Section 37 of the *Health and Safety at Work etc Act 1974* states as follows.

> '(1) Where an offence under any of the relevant statutory provisions committed by a body corporate is proved to have been committed with the consent or connivance of, or to have been attributable to any neglect on the part of, any director, manager, secretary or other similar officer of the body corporate or a person who was purporting to act in any such capacity, he as well as the body corporate shall be guilty of that offence and shall be liable to be proceeded against and punished accordingly.'

Therefore, individual employees can also be liable to an offence under the Regulations, providing the offence was committed with their consent or connivance or was attributable to any neglect on the part of that individual.

Enforcement – Employment Tribunals [7.9]

The enforcement of the Regulations by Employment Tribunals is dependant upon claims by workers and employees being brought to such forums.

Employment Tribunals have been given extended jurisdiction to hear claims arising out of the Regulations and the extent of this new jurisdiction is considered below.

A complaint may be brought by an individual where an employer:

○ fails to allow an individual to exercise a right or receive an entitlement under the Regulations (*Regulation 30*);

○ subjects a worker to suffer a detriment in connection with such worker or employee refusing to forgo his/her rights or entitlements under the Regulations (*Regulation 31*); or

○ dismissing an employee for refusing to forego a right under the Regulations or failing to sign an individual or workforce agreement or being a candidate for or acting as a workforce agreement (*Regulation 32*).

The guidance notes say of Employment Tribunals that they provide:

> 'an informal, accessible means for individuals to assert statutory rights and protections relating to [workers'] statutory rights and protections relating to their employment. The Tribunal generally has three members: a legally qualified chairman and two lay members, one drawn from a panel of employer members and one from a panel of employee members'.

As the guidance notes indicate, Employment Tribunals are aimed at being informal. There is nothing to prevent an employer or an individual worker from representing him/herself at an Employment Tribunal hearing. However, it is common for each party to be represented, whether this be by a lawyer, a trade union official or other person.

Worker's Complaint – Regulation 30 [7.10]

Regulation 30(1) gives a worker the right to present a complaint to an Employment Tribunal where his/her employer has refused to permit him/her to exercise any of the following rights:

○ daily rest of eleven consecutive hours in each 24 hour period (or twelve consecutive hours if it is a young worker) (*Regulation 10(1) and (2)*);

○ an uninterrupted rest period of not less than 24 hours in each seven day period (or 48 hours if it is a young worker) or two uninterrupted rest periods each of not less than 24 hours in each 14 day period or one uninterrupted rest period of not less than 48 hours in each such 14 day period (*Regulations 11(1), (2) and (3)*);

○ failed to provide an in-work rest break where a worker's daily working time is more than six hours (or for young workers where the daily working time is more than 4½ hours) (*Regulations 12(1) and (4)*);

○ failed to give the worker his/her entitlement to annual paid leave of three weeks (*Regulation 13(1)*);

○ failed to pay the worker in respect of the statutory annual leave or compensation related to a payment in lieu of leave arising upon the termination of the worker's engagement (*Regulation 14(2) and 16(1)*);

○ failed to provide a worker with compensatory time off where an adult worker is required by his/her employer to work during a period which would otherwise be a rest period or rest break where such a right has been modified or excluded (*Regulation 24*);

○ failed to provide a young worker in the Armed Forces with an appropriate period of compensatory rest where such a person was required to work during a period which would otherwise be a rest period (*Regulation 25(3)*); or

○ failed to provide a young worker with an equivalent period of compensatory rest within three weeks where the provisions on daily rest and rest breaks for young workers are excluded by virtue of the '*force majeure*' exemption (*Regulation 27(2)* – see 3.19).

Time Limits for Regulation 30 [7.11]

A worker must bring his/her complaint to an Employment Tribunal within three months of the date of the alleged right should have been exercised.

For example, if a worker leaves his/her employer on 1 January 1999 and he/she is entitled to pay in lieu of unused statutory holidays, the worker has until 31 March 1999 to bring a complaint to the Employment Tribunal where the employer failed to make such payments.

Armed Forces [7.12]

Regulation 38(2) makes a special provision of time limits for those workers in the Armed Services. Such workers have an increased time limit of six months in which to bring a claim to an Employment Tribunal. However, this longer period takes into account the fact that a worker in the Armed Services must first:

○ make a complaint in respect of the matter in issue to an officer under the service redress procedure – 'service redress procedures' means such procedures as detailed in *section 190* of the *Army Act*

1955, *section 180* of the *Air Force Act 1955* and *section 130* of the *Naval Discipline Act 1957* respectively; and

○ ensure the complaint has not been withdrawn (i.e. the worker has submitted the complaint to the Defence Council).

In addition, *Regulation 38(2)* states that:

'no complaint concerning the service of any person as a member of the Armed Forces may be presented to an Employment Tribunal under Regulation 30',

unless the two conditions above are satisfied.

The service redress procedures may continue, despite a complaint having been lodged at an Employment Tribunal (*Regulation 38(4)*).

Out of Time Complaints   [7.13]

Regulation 30(2)(b) gives an Employment Tribunal the power to hear a complaint lodged after the three months (or six months) deadline but only:

'within such further period as the tribunal considers reasonable in a case where it is satisfied that *it was not reasonably practicable for the complaint to be presented before the end of that period of three or, as the case may be, six months*' (emphasis added).

Remedies for Regulation 30   [7.14]

Where an Employment Tribunal finds that a complaint arising out of *Regulation 30(1)* is well founded, it may make:

○ a declaration to that effect; and
○ an award of compensation to be paid by the employer to the worker (*Regulation 30(3)*).

In determining what the level of compensation should be, *Regulation 30(4)* states that:

'The amount of the compensation shall be such as the Tribunal considers *just and equitable in all the circumstances* having regard

to –
(a) the employer's default in refusing to permit the worker to exercise his right, and
(b) any loss sustained by the worker which is attributable to the matters complained of' (emphasis added).

The term 'just and equitable' is applied to a number of remedies which the Employment Tribunal may award. It is best known in compensatory awards for unfair dismissal.

Heads of Compensation [7.15]

In determining the loss sustained in cases of unfair dismissal, the heads of compensation which an Employment Tribunal may apply include:

○ loss of earnings;
○ expenses; and
○ compensation for the manner of the dismissal (such awards are rare).

It remains to be seen how an Employment Tribunal may apply such heads (or any other heads) of compensation in relation to *Regulation 30* claims and what level of awards of compensation will be made.

It is worth noting that, unlike unfair dismissal awards for employees and awards for suffering a detriment, where such detriment is the termination of a worker's contract (see 7.19 below), there is no limit on the amount of compensation an Employment Tribunal can award.

Holiday Pay in Lieu [7.16]

The rights to holiday pay in lieu upon termination and annual statutory holiday pay are specifically dealt with under *Regulation 30(5)* which states that:

> 'Where... an Employment Tribunal finds that an employer has failed to pay a worker in accordance with Regulation 14(2) [holiday pay in lieu upon termination] or 16(1) [annual leave holiday pay], it shall order the employer to pay to the worker the amount it finds to be due to him'.

This award of compensation relates strictly to the amount due to the worker as holiday pay. It does not give the Employment Tribunal any scope to exercise its discretion in determining what it considers 'just and equitable in the circumstances'.

The Right Not to Suffer Detriment [7.17]

Workers are given the right not to suffer detriment where such detriment relates to the Regulations.

Regulation 31 inserts *section 45A* into *Part V* of the *ERA 1996. Part V* deals with 'Protection From Suffering Detriment in Employment'.

Section 45A states that a worker has the right not to be subjected to any act or any deliberate failure to act by his/her employer done on the ground that the worker:

'(a) refused (or proposed to refuse) to comply with a requirement which the employer imposed (or proposed to impose) in contravention of the Working Time Regulations 1998;

(b) refused (or proposed to refuse) to forgo a right conferred on him by those Regulations;

(c) failed to sign a workforce agreement for the purposes of these Regulations, or to enter into, or agree to vary or extend, any other agreement with his employer which is provided for in those Regulations;

(d) being –
　(i)　a representative of members of the workforce for the purposes of Schedule 1 to those Regulations [Workforce Agreements], or
　(ii)　a candidate in an election in which any person elected will, on being elected, be such a representative,

(e) brought proceedings against the employer to enforce a right conferred on him by those Regulations, or

(f) alleged that the employer had infringed such a right'.

It would appear that the use of the word 'deliberate' alongside the words 'failure to act' at the outset of *section 45A(1)* means that an employer must 'intend' not to so act if a worker is to be successful in his/her claim.

Should an employer breach the employee's right not to suffer a detriment then, under *section 48(1ZA)* (as inserted by *Regulation 31(2)*), a worker may present a claim to an Employment Tribunal.

The additional provision made by the new section 45A is extended to apply to:

○ the Armed Forces;
○ House of Lords staff; and
○ House of Commons staff.

The restrictions to disclosure of information relating to National security extends to *section 45A* (see *section 202, ERA 1996*).

Section 45A is not extended to Police Officers (see *section 200, ERA 1996*).

What is a 'Detriment' [7.18]

The term 'detriment' should be given a broad meaning, as it encapsulates a wide spectrum of acts and deliberate failures to act.

It may include:

○ demotion;
○ loss of benefits;
○ refusal to promote;
○ loss of pay increases;
○ refusal of training; or
○ termination of employment.

This list is not definitive and case law will certainly increase the instances of recognised acts or omissions which amount to 'detriment'.

An example of 'detriment' is where an employer requests ten of his/her workers to sign up to individual agreements to agree to work more than 48 hours each week. Nine of the workers sign the agreements. When pay rises are given, the nine workers who signed the individual agreements are given pay rises. The individual who refused to work more than 48 hours per week is not given a pay rise. There is no reason for the individual to be refused a pay rise.

On the facts, the worker has a good case to bring a claim to the Employment Tribunal for suffering a detriment. If the worker can show that the reason for him/her not receiving a pay rise is his/her refusal to sign an individual agreement, then he/she will be successful in this claim to have suffered a detriment under the new *section 45A*.

Termination of Contract [7.19]

Where an employee (as opposed to a worker – see 2.17) suffers 'detriment' amounting to termination of his/her contract of employment, then he/she may not claim detriment under *section 45A* but must instead claim unfair dismissal under the new *section 101A, ERA 1996*, as inserted by *Regulation 32* (see 7.25 below). This arises from *section 45A(4)* (inserted by *Regulation 31*) which states that:

> 'This section does not apply where a worker is an employee and the detriment in question amounts to dismissal within the meaning of Part X [unfair dismissal], unless the dismissal is in circumstances in which, by virtue of section 197 [fixed term contracts], Part X does not apply'.

The reference here to *section 197* is to the ability of an employee to contract out of their right to claim unfair dismissal where a fixed term contract comes to an end simply by the fact that it is not renewed.

Section 45A(4) allows an employee to bring a claim for detriment under *section 45A* where a fixed term contract comes to an end in circumstances where they have waived their right to claim unfair dismissal.

Where a worker who is not an employee brings a claim for detriment arising out of termination of employment, *Regulation 31(3)(b)* inserts *section 49(5A)* which provides that the worker's compensation is to be limited to the amount of compensation that would have been awarded if the worker had claimed unfair dismissal.

Section 49(5A) appears to have created an anomaly in the case of employees on fixed term contracts who have waived their right to claim unfair dismissal and therefore may make a claim under *section 45A* on the basis that they have suffered detriment.

Section 49(5A) states that the compensation under *section 45A* will be limited where:

> '(a) the complaint is made under section 48(1ZA);
> (b) the detriment to which the worker is subjected is the termination of his worker's contract, and
> (c) that contract is not a contract of employment'.

It seems damages are not limited in the case of an employee who is entitled to make a claim that he/she has suffered detriment on the expiry of a fixed term contract, as *section 48(1ZA)* only applies where the contract is *not* a contract of employment.

Compensation [7.20]

Where a worker has successfully brought a claim for a breach of his/ her right not to suffer a detriment on the basis of the termination of his/her worker's contract, then the compensation is limited to that which he/she would have received, if he/she had been an employee able to have successfully brought a claim for unfair dismissal.

This ties in together the claims of dismissal by employees and workers and prevents workers obtaining a greater compensation when unlawfully dismissed, i.e. no limit on the award of compensation existing.

Therefore, the worker's compensation is currently limited to the following awards.

○ **Basic award** = Maximum £6,600 (based on the individual's age, length of service and weekly pay (limited to a maximum of £220 gross per week)).
○ **Compensatory award** = Maximum £12,000 (the level of this award is made at the discretion of the Employment Tribunal and will take account of such factors as the likelihood of the individual finding alternative employment and the loss of his/her statutory rights (see the case of *Norton Tool Co Ltd v Tewson [1973] 1 All ER 183*).

The Government has recently stated its intention to review these limits (*Fairness at Work* White Paper).

Perceived Rights or Entitlements [7.21]

If an employer subjects a worker to detriment by reason of the worker relying upon a perceived right or entitlement under the Regulations, it will be immaterial if at a later date it is shown that no such right or entitlement existed. However, the worker must have held in 'good faith' the belief that he/she had such right, or entitlement.

Where a worker alleges that the employer has infringed such a right as contained in *section 45A*, it is sufficient that the worker, without specifying the right, made it reasonably clear to the employer what the right claimed to have been infringed was (*section 45A(3)*).

Remedies for Suffering a Detriment [7.22]

Section 49, ERA 1996 provides that, where an Employment Tribunal finds a complaint under *section 48* to be well founded, the tribunal will:

O   make a declaration to that effect; and
O   may make an award of compensation to be paid by the employer to the worker in respect of the act or failure to act which the complaint relates.

The Employment Tribunal is not under an obligation to make any award of compensation – it is left to its discretion whether or not to make such an award.

If the Employment Tribunal does make an award of compensation, the amount of such compensation will be such as the tribunal considers 'just and equitable' in all the circumstances, having regard to:

O   the infringement to which the complain relates; and
O   any loss which is attributable to the act or failure to act which infringed the worker's right.

Mitigation of Loss [7.23]

There is the common law duty on a worker to mitigate any loss, arising out of a breach of this right by his/her employer.

Further, where an Employment Tribunal finds that a worker is guilty of contributing to the act or failure to act complained of, then the tribunal will reduce the amount of any compensation by such proportion as it considers 'just and equitable'.

Time Limit for Claim of Suffering a Detriment [7.24]

Where a worker wishes to bring a claim that he/she has suffered a detriment in contravention of *section 45A*, he/she has three months starting from the date of the act or deliberate failure to act within which to bring a claim to an Employment Tribunal.

The claim must be brought within three months of the date of the last act or failure to act occurred (*section 48(4), ERA 1996*).

Once again, the Employment Tribunal has the discretion to allow late complaints presented outside the three months' limit where it is satisfied that it was not reasonably practicable for the complaint to be presented within the three months' time limit (*section 48(3), ERA 1996*).

Where an act extends over a period, the 'date of the act' means the last day of that period. A deliberate failure to act is treated as done when it was decided on (*section 48A, ERA 1996*).

Unfair Dismissal [7.25]

Regulation 32 amends the *ERA 1996* to include termination of employees' contracts of employment in connection with working time cases as unfair dismissal.

A new *section 101A* is added to the *ERA 1996* by *Regulation 32*, which states as follows.

> '101A. An employee who is dismissed shall be regarded ... as unfairly dismissed if the reason (or, if more than one, the principal reason) for the dismissal is that the employee –
>
> (a) refused (or proposed to refuse) to comply with a requirement which the employer imposed (or proposed to impose) in contravention of the Working Time Regulations 1998,
>
> (b) refused (or proposed to refuse) to forgo a right conferred on him by those Regulations,
>
> (c) failed to sign a workforce agreement for the purposes of those Regulations, or to enter into, or agree to vary or extend, any other agreement with his employer which is provided for in those Regulations, or
>
> (d) being –
>
> (i) a representative of members of the workforce for the purposes of Schedule 1 to those Regulations, or
>
> (ii) a candidate in an election in which any person elected will, on being elected, be such a representative,

performed (or proposed to perform) any functions or activities as such a representative or candidate.'

Automatic Unfair Dismissal [7.26]

In normal circumstances, where an employee claims for unfair dismissal, he/she is required to:

○ have been continuously employed for a period of not less than two years ending with the effective date of termination; and
○ be under an upper age limit.

However, if an employee is dismissed for an automatically unfair reason, he/she does not have to satisfy these criteria.

A dismissal is automatically unfair if:

○ the reason for selection (or, if more than one reason, the principal reason) an employee is selected for redundancy is one of the grounds set out in 7.26 above;
○ it is shown that the circumstances constituting the redundancy applied equally to one or more other employees in the same undertaking who held positions similar to that held by the employee and who have not been dismissed by the employer; or
○ it is shown that the reason (or, if more than one, the principal reason) for which the employee was selected for dismissal was one of those contained in *section 101A* (see 7.26 above).

Therefore, a new recruit can rely upon *section 101A*, as can an employee who has attained the normal age for retirement in the organisation in which he/she was employed.

Assertion of a Statutory Right [7.27]

Section 104, ERA 1996 protects employees from dismissal for asserting a statutory right. The rights provided by the Regulations are statutory rights for the purposes of *section 104, ERA 1996*.

Section 104 states as follows.

'104 (1) An employee who is dismissed shall be regarded for the purposes of this Part as unfairly dismissed if the reason (or, if more than one, the principal reason) for the dismissal is that the employee –

(a) brought proceedings against the employer to enforce a right of his which is a relevant statutory right, or

(b) alleged that the employer had infringed a right of his which is a relevant statutory right.'

Section 104 goes on to state that it is immaterial whether the employee has a 'working time' right or whether the employer has infringed such a right provided the employee's claim in these instances is made in 'good faith' *(section 104(2))*.

It is sufficient if the employee does not specify the actual right he/she is relying upon but he/she makes it reasonably clear to the employer what the right claimed to have been infringed was.

Time Limit [7.28]

A worker must bring his/her complaint under *section 104, ERA 1996* to an Employment Tribunal within three months of the date of dismissal.

The Employment Tribunal has a discretion to allow claims to proceed after the three months has expired where the employee can show it was not 'reasonably practicable' to bring a claim earlier.

Remedies for a Dismissal for Asserting a Statutory Right [7.29]

An employee who has been dismissed for asserting a statutory right arising out of the Regulations, e.g. refusing to work more than 48 hours each week, may be entitled to the usual basic and compensatory awards made in unfair dismissal cases (see 7.20 above).

Where an individual shows successfully that the reason (or principal reason) for dismissal was for asserting a statutory right arising out of the Regulations, such a dismissal will be automatically unfair (see 7.26).

Once again, there is no requirement on an employee relying upon this provision to:

O have been continuously employed for a period of not less than two years ending with the effective date of termination; or

O be under an upper age limit for bringing a claim.

Appeals [7.30]

Regulation 34 amends *section 21* of the *Employment Tribunals Act 1996*, extending the jurisdiction of the Employment Appeal Tribunal to hear an appeal:

'on any question of law arising from any decision of, or arising in any proceedings before, an Employment Tribunal under or by virtue of … the Working Time Regulations 1998'.

Civil Claims [7.31]

A worker is not precluded by the Regulations from bringing a personal injury claim. This may apply even if a worker agrees in an individual agreement to work more than 48 hours per week (see *Johnston v Bloomsbury Health Authority* at 5.14 above).

A worker may also use a breach of the Regulations in support of a personal injury claim.

Conciliation [7.32]

Conciliation may be used to settle disputes between employees and employers.

Advisory, Conciliation and Arbitration Service [7.33]

Regulation 33 amends *section 18(1)* of the *Employment Tribunals Act 1996*, so it now extends the power of the Advisory, Conciliation and Arbitration Service (ACAS) to include conciliation in relation to matters arising out of *Regulation 30*.

Section 18(3) allows an ACAS officer to promote a settlement before an individual has presented a claim to an Employment Tribunal where either that individual or the person against whom the claim is made invites the ACAS officer to participate in the reaching of a settlement.

Where an individual has presented a claim to an Employment Tribunal, an ACAS officer is under a statutory duty to endeavour to promote a settlement of the proceedings (*section 18(2)* of the *Employment Tribunals Act 1996*).

Restrictions on Contracting Out [7.34]

Regulation 35 deals with the subject of contracting out of a worker's statutory rights and places limitations on when this can be done.

The general rule is that any provision in an agreement (whether a contract of employment or not) is void in so far as it purports to:

O   exclude or limit the operation of any provision of the Regulations, except where the Regulations allow an agreement to have that effect (see Chapter 6) – for example, *Regulation 5* allows an individual to agree to work more than 48 hours per week; or
O   preclude a person bringing a claim under the Regulations before an Employment Tribunal.

Compromise Agreements [7.35]

It is possible to settle a claim arising under *Regulation 30, section 45A, ERA 1996* and *section 101A, ERA 1996* by means of a 'compromise agreement'.

Where a worker does bring a claim or intends to bring a claim before an Employment Tribunal, there are two ways of such a claim being settled.

Where the worker agrees to settle the matter, this can be achieved by either:

O   a settlement by a conciliation officer, recorded in a Form COT3 where the officer has taken action to settle the claim under *section 18* of the *Employment Tribunals Act 1996*; or
O   a compromise agreement is entered into by the worker and the employer.

For a compromise agreement to be binding, the following conditions must be satisfied:

○ the agreement must be in writing;
○ the agreement must relate to the particular complaint;
○ the worker must have received advice from a relevant independent adviser as to the terms and effect of the proposed agreement and, in particular, its effect on his/her ability to pursue his/her rights before an Employment Tribunal;
○ there must be in force, when the adviser gives the advice, a contract of insurance or an indemnity provided for members of a professional body covering the risk of a claim by the worker in respect of loss arising in consequence of the advice;
○ the agreement must identify the adviser; and
○ the agreement must state that the conditions regulating compromise agreements under the Regulations are satisfied (*Regulation 35(3)*).

Regulation 35(4) clarifies who is a 'relevant independent adviser' for the purposes of advising on a compromise agreement. It states the adviser must be:

○ a qualified lawyer – this means:
  • as respects England and Wales, a barrister (whether in practice as such or employed to give legal advice), a solicitor who holds a practising certificate or a person other than a barrister or solicitor who is an authorised advocate or authorised litigator (within the meaning of the *Courts and Legal Services Act 1990*); and
  • as respects Scotland, an advocate (whether in practice as such or employed to give legal advice) or a solicitor who holds a practising certificate;
○ someone who is an officer, official, employee or member of an independent trade union who has been certified in writing by the trade union as competent to give advice and as authorised to do so on behalf of this trade union; or
○ someone who works at an advice centre (whether as an employee or as a volunteer) and has been certified in writing by the centre as competent to give advice and as authorised to do so on behalf of the centre.

Regulation 35(5) states that a person is not a relevant independent adviser when:

○ he/she is employed by or is acting in the matter for the employer or an associated employer – two employers will be 'associated' if:

- ● one is a company or which the other (directly or indirectly) has control; or
- ● both are companies of which a third person (directly or indirectly) has control (*Regulation 3(9)*);
- ○ the trade union or advice centre is the employer, or an associated employer; or
- ○ the worker makes a payment for the advice received from an individual advising at an advice centre.

The Public Interest Disclosure Act 1998   [7.36]

The *Public Interest Disclosure Act 1998* may have an impact on the enforcement of the Regulations by the Health and Safety Executive and the Local Authorities (see 7.2). This arises as, once the Act is in force in its entirety, workers will be encouraged to report their employers' failings and will receive protection for doing so.

This Act received its Royal Assent on 2 July 1998 and will come into force in its entirety in January 1999.

Section 43K of the Act gives a broad definition of the meaning of 'workers' and includes agency workers.

A worker is given protection where he/she makes a 'protected disclosure'.

A disclosure will be 'protected' where the following conditions are satisfied:

- ○ the disclosure must be in the reasonable belief of the worker making the disclosure to show:
  - ● that a criminal offence has been committed, is being committed or is likely to be committed;
  - ● that a person has failed, is failing or is likely to fail to comply with any legal obligation to which he/she is subject;
  - ● that the health or safety of any individual has been or is being or is likely to be endangered; and

- ○ the disclosure must be made in good faith to:
  - ● the worker's employer; or
  - ● to the Health and Safety Executive Inspector or Local Authority Officer where the disclosure relates to any one of the areas for which they have responsibility under the Regulations (see 7.2 above).

Where there is a confidentiality clause in a worker's agreement, such a clause will be void in so far as it purports to preclude a worker from making a protected disclosure.

A worker is given the right not to suffer detriment where he/she makes a protected disclosure. For example, where a worker's contract is terminated by his/her employer and the reason for the termination is the fact that the worker made a protected disclosure, then the worker may bring a claim in the Employment Tribunal.

Where a worker suffers detriment after he/she had made a protected disclosure, compensation will be such amount as the tribunal considers just and equitable in all the circumstances. However, if the detriment suffered is termination then limits apply to the level of compensation.

Where the worker is an employee, the claim will be for unfair dismissal and the amount of compensation will be limited to the usual limits for unfair dismissal compensation (see 7.20 above).

Where the dismissal is of a worker, other than an employee, the limit of compensation that an Employment Tribunal may award is the same as the limit for unfair dismissal compensation (see 7.20).

Appendix 1 – Summary of

Limits and Entitlement	Exclusions and Exceptions (those in bold to be compensated by equivalent periods of rest or afforded appropriate protection)	Reference Period
Working time not to exceed 48 hours in any seven day period.	O Excluded sectors. O Domestic servants. O Those on unmeasured working time. O Employees who have agreed in writing that the limit will not apply (*provided that the employer keeps detailed records*).	Calculated by reference to the average hours worked in any period of 17 weeks (26 weeks in relation to those in other special cases).
Night worker – average hours not to exceed eight in each 24 hour period.	O Excluded sectors. O Domestic servants. O Those on unmeasured working time. O **Other special cases.**	Calculated by reference to the average hours worked in each successive period of 17 weeks.
Night worker – work involving 'special hazards or heavy physical or mental strain' – maximum eight working hours in any 24 hours.	O Excluded sectors. O Domestic servants. O Those on unmeasured working time. O **Other special cases.**	

152

Provisions in the Regulations

Possible Variations by Agreement	Record-Keeping Requirements (Armed Forces excluded)	Penalties
Employees may give seven days' notice to terminate agreement to work in excess of 48 hours. By individual agreement this can be extended to up to three months. Reference periods may be amended to successive periods in a relevant agreement. For reasons which are objective, technical or concern the organisation of work, collective or workforce agreements may vary the 17 week reference period to a period of up to 52 weeks.	Generally must keep records adequate to show the limit complied with and retain for two years. For individual agreements to work in excess of 48 hours to be valid, employers must maintain up to date records of: O each worker who has made an agreement; O the terms of the agreement; O the worker's hours of working-time for the past two years.	Failure to take all reasonable steps to ensure this limit is complied with is a criminal offence. An employee may complain to an Employment Tribunal that he/she has suffered detriment or been unfairly dismissed for failing to agree that the limit will not apply. Dismissal on this basis is automatically unfair.
Collective/workforce agreements may modify or exclude these provisions. Relevant agreements★ may, within limits, set the hours counted as night time. Collective/workforce agreements may determine how many hours during night time a worker must work to be a night worker. May amend reference periods to successive periods in a relevant agreement.	Generally must keep records adequate to show that the limit has been complied with and retain for two years.	Failure to take all reasonable steps to ensure this limit is complied with is a criminal offence. An employee may complain to an Employment Tribunal that he/she has suffered detriment or been unfairly dismissed for failing to agree that the limit will not apply. Dismissal on this basis is automatically unfair.
Collective/workforce agreements may modify or exclude these provisions. Relevant agreements may, within limits, set the hours counted as night time. Collective/workforce agreements may determine how many hours during night time a worker must work to be a night worker. Collective or workforce agreements may identify what is regarded as work of special hazards.	Generally must keep records adequate to show that the limit has been complied with and retain for two years.	Failure to take all reasonable steps to ensure this limit is complied with is a criminal offence. An employee may complain to an Employment Tribunal that he/she has suffered detriment or been unfairly dismissed for failing to agree that the limit will not apply. Dismissal on this basis is automatically unfair.

Limits and Entitlement	**Exclusions and Exceptions** (those in bold to be compensation by equivalent periods of rest or afforded appropriate protection)	**Reference Period**
Night worker – right to health assessment before transfer to night work and then at regular intervals.	O Excluded sectors (except for young workers). O Domestic servants.	
Night worker – duty to transfer to suitable day work on grounds of health problems.	O Excluded sectors. O Domestic servants. O Those on unmeasured working time. O **Other special cases.**	
Duty to provide adequate breaks in monotonous work.	O Excluded sectors. O Domestic servants.	
Daily rest periods – 11 consecutive hours in each 24 hour period (12 hours for young workers)	O Excluded sectors (except young workers). O Those on unmeasured working time (except young workers). O **Other special cases (except young workers).** O **Adult shift workers changing shifts.** O **Adult workers whose work is split up over the day.**	
Weekly rest periods – 24 hours in each seven day period (two days for young workers).	O Excluded sectors (except young workers). O Those on unmeasured working time (except young workers). O **Other special cases (except young workers)** O **Adult shift workers changing shifts.** O **Adult workers whose work is split up over the day.**	
Rest breaks – 20 minutes if working more than six hours (30 minutes if more than 4½ hrs for young workers).	O Excluded sectors (except young workers). O Those on unmeasured working time (except young workers). O **Other special cases (except young workers).**	
Annual leave – three weeks' paid holiday for employees who have worked more than three months (four weeks after 23 November 1999).	O Excluded Sectors.	

Possible Variations by Agreement	Record-Keeping Requirements (Armed Forces excluded)	Penalties
	Must keep records adequate to show this has been complied with and retain for two years.	Failure to take all reasonable steps to ensure this is complied with is a criminal offence.
Collective/workforce agreements may modify or exclude these provisions.		Failure to take all reasonable steps to ensure this limit is complied with is a criminal offence.
		Failure to take all reasonable steps to ensure this is complied with is a criminal offence.
Collective/workforce agreements may modify or exclude these provisions (except young workers).		An employee may bring a complaint in an Employment Tribunal that he/she has not been allowed to exercise this right or has suffered detriment for refusing to forgo it. An Employment Tribunal may award damages if the complaint is well founded.
Collective/workforce agreements may modify or exclude these provisions (except young workers). A relevant agreement may establish when each period of seven or fourteen days is to begin.		An employee may bring a complaint in an Employment Tribunal that he/she has not been allowed to exercise this right or has suffered detriment for refusing to forgo it. An Employment Tribunal may award damages if the complaint is well founded.
Collective/workforce agreements may modify or exclude these provisions and duration and terms of rest breaks can be set by collective/workforce agreement (except young workers).		An employee may bring a complaint in an Employment Tribunal that he/she has not been allowed to exercise this right or has suffered detriment for refusing to forgo it. The Tribunal may award damages if the complaint is well founded.
Relevant agreements may specify when a leave year may begin.		An employee may bring a complaint in an Employment Tribunal that he/she has not been allowed to exercise this right or has suffered detriment for refusing to forgo it and that he/she has not received holiday pay. The Tribunal may award damages if the complaint is well founded.

Appendix 2 – Full and Partial Exemptions

	Exceptions from the Provisions			
EXCEPTED CATEGORIES	**Excluded Sectors** Air, Rail, Road, Doctors in training etc (*Regulation 18*)	**Domestic Service** (*Regulation 19*)	**Unmeasured Working Time** (*Regulation 20*)	**Other Special Cases★** e.g. distant workers, security work, continuous service etc (*Regulation 21*)
48-hour week (*Regulations 4(1)* and *(2)*).	✓	✓	✓	
Limit of an average eight hours for night work (*Regulations 6(1)* and *(2)*).	✓	✓	✓	✓
Limit of eight hours for night work involving special hazards (*Regulation 6(7)*).	✓	✓	✓	✓
Health assessment for night workers (*Regulation 7(1)*).	✓	✓		
Health and capabilities assessment for young workers working at night (*Regulation 7(2)*).		✓		
Transferring ill night worker to day work (*Regulation 7(6)*).	✓	✓		
Adequate rest breaks in monotonous or pre-determined work (*Regulation 8*).	✓	✓		
Entitlement to daily rest adult workers (*Regulation 10(1)*).	✓		✓	✓
Entitlement to daily rest young workers (*Regulation 10(2)*).				
Entitlement to weekly rest (*Regulations 11(1)* and *(2)*).	✓		✓	✓
Enititlement to weekly rest young workers (*Regulations 11(3)*).				
In work rest break young workers (*Regulation 12(4)*).				
In-work rest break adult workers (*Regulation 12(1)*).	✓		✓	✓
Annual leave entitlement (*Regulation 13*).	✓			
Payment for holiday leave (*Regulation 16*).	✓			

*NOTE: Where the application of any provision of these Regulations is excluded and a worker is accordingly required to work during a rest period, an employer will either:

O grant to the worker an equivalent period of compensatory rest; or (if this is not possible for objective reasons)

O afford the worker such protection as may be appropriate to safeguard the worker's health and safety, e.g. increase the number of 'in work' breaks and the number of health check.

Which Workers are Subject to Exemptions?

Excluded Sectors

The following sectors are 'excluded sectors' for the purposes of exceptions to the Regulations:

O air, rail, road, sea, inland waterway and lake transport;
O sea fishing;
O other work at sea;
O to the activities of doctors in training; and
O where characteristics peculiar to certain specified services, such as the Armed Forces or the police, or to certain specific activities in the civil protection services, inevitably conflict with the provisions of these Regulations.

Domestic Service

The term 'domestic service' means a worker employed as a domestic servant in a private household.

Unmeasured Working Time

The term 'unmeasured working time' applies to a worker where, on account of the specific characteristics of the activity in which he/she is engaged, the duration of his/her working time is not measured or predetermined or can be determined by the worker him/herself, as may be the case for:

O managing executives or other persons with autonomous decision-taking powers;
O family workers; or
O workers officiating at religious ceremonies in churches and religious communities.

157

'Other Special Cases'

The following are considered 'special cases' for the purposes of exceptions to the Regulations.

○ Where the worker's activities are such that his/her place of work and place of residence are distant from one another or his/her different places of work are distant from one another.

○ Where the worker is engaged in security and surveillance activities requiring a permanent presence in order to protect property and persons, as may be the case for security guards and caretakers or security firms.

○ Where a conciliation officer has taken action to settle the claim under *section 18* of the *Employment Tribunals Act 1996.* here the worker's activities involve the need for continuity of service or production, as may be the case in relation to:

- services relating to the reception, treatment or care provided by hospitals or similar establishments, residential institutions and prisons;
- work at docks or airports;
- press, radio, television, cinematographic production, postal and telecommunications services and civil protection services;
- gas, water and electricity production, transmission and distribution, household refuse collection and incineration;
- industries in which work cannot be interrupted on technical grounds;
- research and development activities; and
- agriculture.

○ Where there is a foreseeable surge of activity, as may be the case in relation to:

- agriculture;
- tourism; and
- postal services.

○ Where the worker's activities are affected by:

- an occurrence due to unusual and unforseeable circumstances, beyond the control of the worker's employer;
- exceptional events, the consequences of which could not have been avoided despite the exercise of all due care by the employer; or
- an accident or the imminent risk of an accident.

Appendix 3 – Record-Keeping

The following checklist details those areas where an employer is obliged to keep records.

Limit	Nature of Duty	Time Limit Over Which Records Must Be Kept
Maximum 48 hour average working week (*Regulation 4(1)*).	Records adequate to show whether limits have been complied with.	Retain for two years from date on which they were made.
Maximum 48 hour average working week (*Regulation 4(1)*) in respect of workers who have agreed to work in excess of 48 hours.	Records which specify: ○ identity of each such worker; ○ terms of agreements; and ○ the number of hours worked in each reference period.	Records to be kept for each reference period since the agreement came into force (excluding any period ending more than two years before most recent entry).
Average of eight normal working hours for night workers (*Regulation 6(1)*).	Records adequate to show whether limits have been complied with.	Retain for two years from date on which they were made.
Maximum eight hours working hours in any 24 for night-workers with work involving special hazards (*Regulation 6(7)*).	Records adequate to show whether limits have been complied with.	Retain for two years from date on which they were made.
Free health assessments for adult workers (Regulation 7(1)).	Records adequate to show whether limits have been complied with.	Retain for two years from date on which they were made.
Free health and capacities assessments for young workers (*Regulation 7(2)*).	Records adequate to show whether limits have been complied with.	Retain for two years from date on which they were made.

Appendix 4 – Agreements

Which agreements can be used to modify or exclude various provisions of the Regulations?

Working Time

To add to the definition of working time.

---

48 Hour Working Week

Agreement to work in excess of 48 hours.

Notice period for worker to terminate agreement to work in excess of 48 hours.

Amendment of reference periods to successive period rather than rolling period.

Amendment of reference period to alternate length period of up to 52 weeks (for objective or technical reasons or reasons concerning the organisation of work, including for new joiners).

Length Of Night Work

Exclude or modify application of Regulations in relation to average normal hours of a night worker.

Exclude or modify application of Regulations in relation to maximum working hours or those night workers whose work involves work of special hazards.

Vary definition of night time.

Amend reference period to successive periods rather than rolling periods.

Set the definition of night worker.

Identify work regarded as involving special hazards or heavy physical or mental strain.

to Exclude Provisions

Individual Agreement (No contractual force required)	Contractually Binding Agreement Between Worker & Employer	Collective Agreement	Workforce Agreement
	✓	✓	✓
✓			
✓			
	✓	✓	✓
		✓	✓
		✓	✓
		✓	✓
	✓	✓	✓
	✓	✓	✓
		✓	✓
		✓	✓

Rest Periods
Modify or exclude entitlement of adults to a daily rest period of 11 consecutive hours.★
Modify or exclude weekly rest period for adult workers.★
Determine upon which day of the week the reference periods of 7 or 14 days will start for the weekly rest period.
Rest Breaks
Modify, exclude or set the duration and terms of adult workers entitlement to a rest break.
Annual Leave
Set leave year.
Determine the calculation of the payment on termination payable by the employer or the worker.
Amend the notice provision to annual leave.

★ Note: Where the application of any provision of the Regulations is excluded and a worker is accordingly required to work during a rest period, an employer will either:
○   grant to the worker an equivalent period of compansatory rest; or (if this is not possible for objective reasons)
○   afford the worker such protection as may be appropriate to safeguard the worker's health and safety, e.g. increase the number of 'in work' breaks and the number of health checks.

Individual Agreement (No contractual force required)	Contractually Binding Agreement Between Worker and Employer	Collective Agreement	Workforce Agreement
		✓	✓
		✓	✓
	✓	✓	✓
		✓	✓
	✓	✓	✓
	✓	✓	✓
	✓	✓	✓

European Working Time Directive

Preamble

SECTION I – SCOPE AND DEFINITIONS
Article 1 – Purpose and scope
Article 2 – Definitions

SECTION II – MINIMUM REST PERIODS – OTHER
ASPECTS OF THE ORGANISATION OF WORKING TIME
Article 3 – Daily rest
Article 4 – Breaks
Article 5 – Weekly rest period
Article 6 – Maximum weekly working time
Article 7 – Annual leave

SECTION III – NIGHT WORK SHIFT – WORK – PATTERNS
OF WORK
Article 8 – Length of night work
Article 9 – Health assessment and transfer of night workers to
day work
Article 10 – Guarantees for night-time working
Article 11 – Notification of regular use of night workers
Article 12 – Safety and health protection
Article 13 – Pattern of work

SECTION IV – MISCELLANEOUS PROVISIONS
Article 14 – More specific Community provisions
Article 15 – More favourable provisions
Article 16 – Reference periods
Article 17 – Derogations
Article 18 – Final provisions

COUNCIL DIRECTIVE No 93/104/EC of 23 November 1993 concerning certain aspects of the organisation of working time

THE COUNCIL OF THE EUROPEAN UNION,

Having regard to the Treaty establishing the European Community, and in particular Article 118a thereof,

Having regard to the proposal from the Commission[1],

In cooperation with the European Parliament[2],

Having regard to the opinion of the Economic and Social Committee[3],

Whereas Article 118a of the Treaty provides that the Council shall adopt, by means of directives, minimum requirements for encouraging improvements, especially in the working environment, to ensure a better level of protection of the safety and health of workers;

Whereas, under the terms of that Article, those directives are to avoid imposing administrative, financial and legal constraints in a way which would hold back the creation and development of small and medium-sized undertakings;

Whereas the provisions of Council Directive 89/391/EEC of 12 June 1989 on the introduction of measures to encourage improvements in the safety and health of workers at work[4] are fully applicable to the areas covered by this Directive without prejudice to more stringent and/or specific provisions contained therein;

Whereas the Community Charter of the Fundamental Social Rights of Workers, adopted at the meeting of the European Council held at Strasbourg on 9 December 1989 by the Heads of State or of Government of 11 Member States, and in particular points 7, first subparagraph, 8 and 19, first subparagraph, thereof, declared that:

'7. The completion of the internal market must lead to an improvement in the living and working conditions of workers in the European Community. This process must result from an approximation of these conditions while the improvement is being maintained, as regards in particular the duration and organisation of working time and forms of employment other than open-ended contracts, such as fixed-term contracts, part-time working, temporary work and seasonal work.

8. Every worker in the European Community shall have a right to a weekly rest period and to annual paid leave, the duration of which must be progressively harmonised in accordance with national practices.

19. Every worker must enjoy satisfactory health and safety conditions in his working environment. Appropriate measures must be taken in order to achieve further harmonisation of conditions in this area while maintaining the improvements made.';

Whereas the improvement of workers' safety, hygiene and health at work is an objective which should not be subordinated to purely economic considerations;

Whereas this Directive is a practical contribution towards creating the social dimension of the internal market;

Whereas laying down minimum requirements with regard to the organisation of working time is likely to improve the working conditions of workers in the Community;

Whereas, in order to ensure the safety and health of Community workers, the latter must be granted minimum daily, weekly and annual periods of rest and adequate breaks; whereas it is also necessary in this context to place a maximum limit on weekly working hours;

Whereas account should be taken of the principles of the International Labour Organisation with regard to the organisation of working time, including those relating to night-work;

Whereas, with respect to the weekly rest period, due account should be taken of the diversity of cultural, ethnic, religious and other factors in the Member States; whereas, in particular, it is ultimately for each Member State to decide whether Sunday should be included in the weekly rest period, and if so to what extent;

Whereas research has shown that the human body is more sensitive at night to environmental disturbances and also to certain burdensome forms of work organisation and that long periods of night work can be detrimental to the health of workers and can endanger safety at the workplace;

Whereas there is a need to limit the duration of periods of night work, including overtime, and to provide for employers who regularly use night workers to bring this information to the attention of the competent authorities if they so request;

Whereas it is important that night workers should be entitled to a free health assessment prior to their assignment and thereafter at regular intervals and that whenever possible they should be transferred to day work for which they are suited if they suffer from health problems;

Whereas the situation of night and shift workers requires that the level of safety and health protection should be adapted to the nature of their work and that the organisation and functioning of protection and prevention services and resources should be efficient;

Whereas specific working conditions may have detrimental effects on the safety and health of workers; whereas the organisation of work according to a certain pattern must take account of the general principle of adapting work to the worker;

Whereas, given the specific nature of the work concerned, it may be necessary to adopt separate measures with regard to the organisation of working time in certain sectors or activities which are excluded from the scope of this Directive;

Whereas, in view of the question likely to be raised by the organisation of working time within an undertaking, it appears desirable to provide for flexibility in the application of certain provisions of this Directive, whilst ensuring compliance with the principles of protecting the safety and health of workers;

Whereas it is necessary to provide that certain provisions may be subject to derogations implemented, according to the case, by the Member States or the two sides of industry; whereas, as a general rule, in the event of a derogation, the workers concerned must be given equivalent compensatory rest periods,

HAS ADOPTED THIS DIRECTIVE:

NOTES
[1] OJ C254, 9.10.90, p 4.
[2] OJ C72, 18.3.91, p 95; and Decision of 27 October 1993 (not yet published in the Official Journal).
[3] OJ C60, 8.3.91, p 26.
[4] OJ L183, 29.6.89, p 1.

SECTION I – SCOPE AND DEFINITIONS

Article 1 – Purpose and scope

1. This Directive lays down minimum safety and health requirements for the organisation of working time.

2. This Directive applies to –
(a) minimum periods of daily rest, weekly rest and annual leave, to breaks and maximum weekly working time; and
(b) certain aspects of night work, shift work and patterns of work.

3. This Directive shall apply to all sectors of activity, both public and private, within the meaning of Article 2 of Directive 89/391/EEC, without prejudice to Article 17 of this Directive, with the exception of air, rail, road, sea, inland waterway and lake transport, sea fishing, other work at sea and the activities of doctors in training;

4. The provisions of Directive 89/391/EEC are fully applicable to the matters referred to in paragraph 2, without prejudice to more stringent and/or specific provisions contained in this Directive.

Article 2 – Definitions

For the purposes of this Directive, the following definitions shall apply –

1. *working time* shall mean any period during which the worker is working, at the employer's disposal and carrying out his activity or duties, in accordance with national laws and/or practice;

2. *rest period* shall mean any period which is not working time;

3. *night time* shall mean any period of not less than seven hours, as defined by national law; and which must include in any case the period between midnight and 5 am;

4. *night worker* shall mean –
(a) on the one hand, any worker, who, during night time, works at least three hours of his daily working time as a normal course; and
(b) on the other hand, any worker who is likely during night time to work a certain proportion of his annual working time, as defined at the choice of the Member State concerned –
(i) by national legislation, following consultation with the two sides of industry; or
(ii) by collective agreements or agreements concluded between the two sides of industry at national or regional level;

5. *shift work* shall mean any method of organising work in shifts whereby workers succeed each other at the same work stations according to a certain pattern, including a rotating pattern, and which may be continuous or discontinuous, entailing the need for workers to work at different times over a given period of days or weeks;

6. *shift worker* shall mean any worker whose work schedule is part of shift work.

SECTION II – MINIMUM REST PERIODS – OTHER ASPECTS OF THE ORGANISATION OF WORKING TIME

Article 3 – Daily rest

Member States shall take the measures necessary to ensure that every worker is entitled to a minimum daily rest period of 11 consecutive hours per 24-hour period.

Article 4 – Breaks

Member States shall take the measures necessary to ensure that, where the working day is longer than six hours, every worker is entitled to a rest break, the details of which, including duration and the terms on which it is granted, shall be laid down in collective agreements or agreements between the two sides of industry or, failing that, by national legislation.

Article 5 – Weekly rest period

Member States shall take the measures necessary to ensure that, per each seven-day period, every worker is entitled to a minimum uninterrupted rest period of 24 hours plus the 11 hours' daily rest referred to in Article 3.

[The minimum rest period referred to in the first subparagraph shall in principle include Sunday.]

If objective, technical or work organisation conditions so justify, a minimum rest period of 24 hours may be applied.

Article 6 – Maximum weekly working time

Member States shall take the measures necessary to ensure that, in keeping with the need to protect the safety and health of workers –

1. the period of weekly working time is limited by means of laws, regulations or administrative provisions or by collective agreements or agreements between the two sides of industry;

2. the average working time for each seven-day period, including overtime, does not exceed 48 hours.

Article 7 – Annual leave

1. Member States shall take the measures necessary to ensure that every worker is entitled to paid annual leave of at least four weeks in accordance with the conditions for entitlement to, and granting of, such leave laid down by national legislation and/or practice.
2. The minimum period of paid annual leave may not be replaced by an allowance in lieu, except where the employment relationship is terminated.

SECTION III – NIGHT WORK – SHIFT WORK – PATTERNS OF WORK

Article 8 – Length of night work

Member States shall take the measures necessary to ensure that:

1. normal hours of work for night workers do not exceed an average of eight hours in any 24-hour period;

2. night workers whose work involves special hazards or heavy physical or mental strain do not work more than eight hours in any period of 24 hours during which they perform night work.

For the purposes of the aforementioned, work involving special hazards or heavy physical or mental strain shall be defined by national legislation and/or practice or by collective agreements or agreements concluded between the two sides of industry, taking account of the specific effects and hazards of night work.

Article 9 – Health assessment and transfer of night workers to day work

1. Member States shall take the measures necessary to ensure that:
(a) night workers are entitled to a free health assessment before their assignment and thereafter at regular intervals;
(b) night workers suffering from health problems recognised as being

connected with the fact that they perform night work are transferred whenever possible to day work to which they are suited.

2. The free health assessment referred to in paragraph 1(a) must comply with medical confidentiality.

3. The free health assessment referred to in paragraph 1(a) may be conducted within the national health system.

Article 10 – Guarantees for night-time working

Member States may make the work of certain categories of night workers subject to certain guarantees, under conditions laid down by national legislation and/or practice, in the case of workers who incur risks to their safety or health linked to night-time working.

Article 11 – Notification of regular use of night workers

Member States shall take the measures necessary to ensure that an employer who regularly uses night workers brings this information to the attention of the competent authorities if they so request.

Article 12 – Safety and health protection

Member States shall take the measures necessary to ensure that:

1. night workers and shift workers have safety and health protection appropriate to the nature of their work;

2. appropriate protection and prevention services or facilities with regard to the safety and health of night workers and shift workers are equivalent to those applicable to other workers and are available at all times.

Article 13 – Pattern of work

Member States shall take the measures necessary to ensure that an employer who intends to organise work according to a certain pattern takes account of the general principle of adapting work to the worker, with a view, in particular, to alleviating monotonous work and work at a predetermined work-rate, depending on the type of activity, and of safety and health requirements, especially as regards breaks during working time.

SECTION IV – MISCELLANEOUS PROVISIONS

Article 14 – More specific Community provisions

The provisions of this Directive shall not apply where other Community instruments contain more specific requirements concerning certain occupations or occupational activities.

Article 15 – More favourable provisions

This Directive shall not affect Member States' right to apply or introduce laws, regulations or administrative provisions more favourable to the protection of the safety and health of workers or to facilitate or permit the application of collective agreements or agreements concluded between the two sides of industry which are more favourable to the protection of the safety and health of workers.

Article 16 – Reference periods

Member States may lay down –

1. for the application of Article 5 (weekly rest period), a reference period not exceeding 14 days;

2. for the application of Article 6 (maximum weekly working time), a reference period not exceeding four months.

The periods of paid annual leave, granted in accordance with Article 7, and the periods of sick leave shall not be included or shall be neutral in the calculation of the average;

3. for the application of Article 8 (length of night work), a reference period defined after consultation of the two sides of industry or by collective agreements or agreements concluded between the two sides of industry at national or regional level.

If the minimum weekly rest period of 24 hours required by Article 5 falls within that reference period, it shall not be included in the calculation of the average.

Article 17 – Derogations

1. With due regard for the general principles of the protection of the safety and health of workers, Member States may derogate from Article 3,

4, 5, 6, 8 or 16 when, on account of the specific characteristics of the activity concerned, the duration of the working time is not measured and/or predetermined or can be determined by the workers themselves, and particularly in the case of:

(a) managing executives or other persons with autonomous decision-taking powers;
(b) family workers; or
(c) workers officiating at religious ceremonies in churches and religious communities.

2. Derogations may be adopted by means of laws, regulations or administrative provisions or by means of collective agreements or agreements between the two sides of industry provided that the workers concerned are afforded equivalent periods of compensatory rest or that, in exceptional cases in which it is not possible, for objective reasons, to grant such equivalent periods of compensatory rest, the workers concerned are afforded appropriate protection:

2.1 from Articles 3, 4, 5, 8 and 16:

(a) in the case of activities where the worker's place of work and his place of residence are distant from one another or where the worker's different places of work are distant from one another;
(b) in the case of security and surveillance activities requiring a permanent presence in order to protect property and persons, particularly security guards and caretakers or security firms;
(c) in the case of activities involving the need for continuity of service or production, particularly –
  (i)   services relating to the reception, treatment and/or care provided by hospitals or similar establishments, residential institutions and prisons;
  (ii)   dock or airport workers;
  (iii) press, radio, television, cinematographic production, postal and telecommunications services, ambulance, fire and civil protection services;
  (iv) gas, water and electricity production, transmission and distribution, household refuse collection and incineration plants;
  (v)   industries in which work cannot be interrupted on technical grounds;
  (vi) research and development activities;
  (v)   agriculture;
(d) where there is a foreseeable surge of activity, particularly in –
  (i)   agriculture;

      (ii)   tourism;
      (iii) postal services;

2.2. from Articles 3, 4, 5, 8 and 16:

(a)   in the circumstances described in Article 5(4) of Directive 89/391/
       EEC;
(b)   in cases of accident or imminent risk of accident;

2.3. from Articles 3 and 5:

(a)   in the case of shift work activities, each time the worker changes
       shift and cannot take daily and/or weekly rest periods between the
       end of one shift and the start of the next one;
(b)   in the case of activities involving periods of work split up over the
       day, particularly those of cleaning staff.

3. Derogations may be made from Articles 3, 4, 5, 8 and 16 by means of collective agreements or agreements concluded between the two sides of industry at national or regional level or, in conformity with the rules laid down by them, by means of collective agreements or agreements concluded between the two sides of industry at a lower level.

Member States in which there is no statutory system ensuring the conclusion of collective agreements or agreements concluded between the two sides of industry at national or regional level, on the matters covered by this Directive, or those Member States in which there is a specific legislative framework for this purpose and within the limits thereof, may, in accordance with national legislation and/or practice, allow derogations from Articles 3, 4, 5, 8 and 16 by way of collective agreements or agreements concluded between the two sides of industry at the appropriate collective level.

The derogations provided for in the first and second subparagraphs shall be allowed on condition that equivalent compensating rest periods are granted to the workers concerned or, in exceptional cases where it is not possible for objective reasons to grant such periods, the workers concerned are afforded appropriate protection.

Member States may lay down rules:

 – for the application of this paragraph by the two sides of industry, and
 – for the extension of the provisions of collective agreements or agreements concluded in conformity with this paragraph to other workers in accordance with national legislation and/or practice.

4. The option to derogate from point 2 of Article 16, provided in paragraph 2, points 2.1. and 2.2. and in paragraph 3 of this Article, may not result in the establishment of a reference period exceeding six months.

However, Member States shall have the option, subject to compliance with the general principles relating to the protection of the safety and health of workers, of allowing, for objective or technical reasons or reasons concerning the organisation of work, collective agreements or agreements concluded between the two sides of industry to set reference periods in no event exceeding 12 months.

Before the expiry of a period of seven years from the date referred to in Article 18(1)(a), the Council shall, on the basis of a Commission proposal accompanied by an appraisal report, re-examine the provisions of this paragraph and decide what action to take.

Article 18 – Final provisions

1. (a) Member States shall adopt the laws, regulations and administrative provisions necessary to comply with this Directive by 23 November 1996, or shall ensure by that date that the two sides of industry establish the necessary measures by agreement, with Member States being obliged to take any necessary steps to enable them to guarantee at all times that the provisions laid down by this Directive are fulfilled.

(b) (i) However, a Member State shall have the option not to apply Article 6, while respecting the general principles of the protection of the safety and health of workers, and provided it takes the necessary measures to ensure that:

– no employer requires a worker to work more than 48 hours over a seven-day period, calculated as an average for the reference period referred to in point 2 of Article 16, unless he has first obtained the worker's agreement to perform such work,

– no worker is subjected to any detriment by his employer because he is not willing to give his agreement to perform such work,

– the employer keeps up-to-date records of all workers who carry out such work,

– the records are placed at the disposal of the competent authorities, which may, for reasons connected with the safety and/or health of workers, prohibit or restrict the possibility of exceeding the maximum weekly working hours,

– the employer provides the competent authorities at their request with information on cases in which agreement has been given by workers to perform work exceeding 48 hours over a period of seven days, calculated as an average for the reference period referred to in point 2 of Article 16.

Before the expiry of a period of seven years from the date referred to in (a), the Council shall, on the basis of a Commission proposal accompanied by an appraisal report, re-examine the provisions of this point (i) and decide on what action to take.

(ii) Similarly, Member States shall have the option, as regards the application of Article 7, of making use of a transitional period of not more than three years from the date referred to in (a), provided that during that transitional period –

– every worker receives three weeks' paid annual leave in accordance with the conditions for the entitlement to, and granting of, such leave laid down by national legislation and/or practice, and

– the three-week period of paid annual leave may not be replaced by an allowance in lieu, except where the employment relationship is terminated.

(c) Member states shall forthwith inform the Commission thereof.

2. When Member States adopt the measures referred to in paragraph 1, they shall contain a reference to this Directive or shall be accompanied by such reference on the occasion of their official publication. The methods of making such a reference shall be laid down by the Member States.

3. Without prejudice to the right of Member States to develop, in the light of changing circumstances, different legislative, regulatory or contractual provisions in the field of working time, as long as the minimum requirements provided for in this Directive are complied with, implementation of this Directive shall not constitute valid grounds for reducing the general level of protection afforded to workers.

4. Member States shall communicate to the Commission the texts of the provisions of national law already adopted or being adopted in the field governed by this Directive.

5. Member States shall report to the Commission every five years on the practical implementation of the provisions of this Directive, indicating the viewpoints of the two sides of industry.

The Commission shall inform the European Parliament, the Council, the Economic and Social Committee and the Advisory Committee on Safety, Hygiene and Health Protection at Work thereof.

6. Every five years the Commission shall submit to the European Parliament, the Council and the Economic and Social Committee a report on the application of this Directive taking into account paragraphs 1, 2, 3, 4 and 5.

Article 19

This Directive is addressed to the Member States.

Done at Brussels, 23 November 1993.

For the Council

The President

M.Smet

1998 No. 1833

TERMS AND CONDITIONS OF EMPLOYMENT

The Working Time Regulations 1998

Made	*30th July 1998*
Laid before Parliament	*30th July 1998*
Coming into force	*1st October 1998*

ARRANGEMENT OF REGULATIONS

PART I
GENERAL

1. Citation, commencement and extent
2. Interpretation

PART II
RIGHTS AND OBLIGATIONS CONCERNING WORKING TIME

3. General
4. Maximum weekly working time
5. Agreement to exclude the maximum
6. Length of night work
7. Health assessment and transfer of night workers to day work
8. Pattern of work
8. Records
9. Daily rest
10. Weekly rest period
11. Rest breaks
12. Entitlement to annual leave
13. Compensation related to entitlement to leave
14. Dates on which leave is taken
15. Payment in respect of periods of leave
16. Entitlements under other provisions

PART III
EXCEPTIONS

18. Excluded sectors
19. Domestic service
20. Unmeasured working time

21. Other special cases
22. Shift workers
23. Collective and workforce agreements
24. Compensatory rest
25. Workers in the armed forces
26. Young workers: *force majeure*
27. Young workers employed on ships

PART IV

MISCELLANEOUS

28. Enforcement
29. Offences
30. Remedies
31. Right not to suffer detriment
32. Unfair dismissal
33. Conciliation
34. Appeals
35. Restrictions on contracting out

PART V

SPECIAL CLASSES OF PERSON

36. Agency workers not otherwise 'workers'
37. Crown employment
38. Armed forces
39. House of Lords staff
40. House of Commons staff
41. Police service
42. Non-employed trainees
43. Agricultural workers

SCHEDULES

1. Workforce agreements
2. Workers employed in agriculture

The Secretary of State, being a Minister designated for the purposes of section 2(2) of the European Communities Act 1972[1] in relation to measures relating to the organization of working time[2] and measures relating to the employment of children and young persons[3], in exercise of the powers conferred on him by that provision hereby makes the following Regulations –

---

1. 1972 c.68.
2. SI 1997/1174.
3. SI 1996/266.

PART I
GENERAL

Citation, commencement and extent

1. – (1) These Regulations may be cited as the Working Time Regulations 1998 and shall come into force on 1st October 1998.

(2) These Regulations extend to Great Britain only.

Interpretation

2. – (1) In these Regulations –

'the 1996 Act' means the Employment Rights Act 1996;[1]

'adult worker' means a worker who has attained the age of 18;

'the armed forces' means any of the naval, military and air forces of the Crown;

'calendar year' means the period of twelve months beginning with 1st January in any year;

'the civil protection services' includes the police, fire brigades and ambulance services, the security and intelligence services, customs and immigration officers, the prison service, the coastguard, and lifeboat crew and other voluntary rescue services;

'collective agreement' means a collective agreement within the meaning of section 178 of the Trade Union and Labour Relations (Consolidation) Act 1992,[2] the trade union parties to which are independent trade unions within the meaning of section 5 of that Act;

'day' means a period of 24 hours beginning at midnight;

'employer', in relation to a worker, means the person by whom the worker is (or, where the employment has ceased, was) employed;

'employment', in relation to a worker, means employment under his contract, and 'employed' shall be construed accordingly;

'night time', in relation to a worker, means a period –

(a)   the duration of which is not less than seven hours, and

(b)   which includes the period between midnight and 5 am,

which is determined for the purposes of these Regulations by a relevant agreement, or, in default of such a determination, the period between 11 pm and 6 am;

'night work' means work during night time;

'night worker' means a worker –

(a)   who, as a normal course, works at least three hours of his daily working time during night time, or

(b)   who is likely, during night time, to work at least such proportion of his annual working time as may be specified for the purposes of these Regulations in a collective agreement or a workforce agreement;

and, for the purpose of paragraph (a) of this definition, a person works hours as a normal course (without prejudice to the generality of that expression) if he works such hours on the majority of days on which he works;

'relevant agreement', in relation to a worker, means a workforce agreement which applies to him, any provision of a collective agreement which forms part of a contract between him and his employer, or any other agreement in writing which is legally enforceable as between the worker and his employer;

'relevant training' means work experience provided pursuant to a training course or programme, training for employment, or both, other than work experience or training –

- (a)   the immediate provider of which is an educational institution or a person whose main business is the provision of training, and
- (b)   which is provided on a course run by that institution or person;

'rest period', in relation to a worker, means a period which is not working time, other than a rest break or leave to which the worker is entitled under these Regulations;

'worker' means an individual who has entered into or works under (or, where the employment has ceased, worked under) –

- (a)   a contract of employment; or
- (b)   any other contract, whether express or implied and (if it is express) whether oral or in writing, whereby the individual undertakes to do or perform personally any work or services for another party to the contract whose status is not by virtue of the contract that of a client or customer of any profession or business undertaking carried on by the individual;

and any reference to a worker's contract shall be construed accordingly;

'worker employed in agriculture' has the same meaning as in the Agricultural Wages Act 1948[3] or the Agricultural Wages (Scotland) Act 1949[4], and a reference to a worker partly employed in agriculture is to a worker employed in agriculture whose employer also employs him for non-agricultural purposes;

'workforce agreement' means an agreement between an employer and workers employed by him or their representatives in respect of which the conditions set out in Schedule 1 to these Regulations are satisfied;

'working time', in relation to a worker, means –

- (a)   any period during which he is working, at his employer's disposal and carrying out his activity or duties,
- (b)   any period during which he is receiving relevant training, and
- (c)   any additional period which is to be treated as working time for the purpose of these Regulations under a relevant agreement;

and 'work' shall be construed accordingly;

'Working Time Directive' means Council Directive 93/104/EC of 23rd November 1993 concerning certain aspects of the organization of working time[5];

'young worker' means a worker who has attained the age of 15 but not the age of 18 and who, as respects England and Wales, is over compulsory school age (construed in accordance with section 8 of the Education Act 1996)[6] and, as respects Scotland, is over school age (construed in accordance with section 31 of the Education (Scotland) Act 1980)[7], and

'Young Workers Directive' means Council Directive 94/33/EC of 22nd June 1994 on the protection of young people at work.[8]

(2) In the absence of a definition in these Regulations, words and expressions used in particular provisions which are also used in corresponding provisions of the Working Time Directive or the Young Workers Directive have the same meaning as they have in those corresponding provisions.

(3) In these Regulations –

    (a)   a reference to a numbered regulation is to the regulation in these Regulations bearing that number;

    (b)   a reference in a regulation to a numbered paragraph is to the paragraph in that regulation bearing that number; and

    (c)   a reference in a paragraph to a lettered sub-paragraph is to the sub-paragraph in that paragraph bearing that letter.

---

1. 1996 c.18.
2. 1992 c.52.
3. 1948 c.47.
4. 1949 c.30.
5. O.J. No. L307, 13.12.93, p.18.
6. 1996 c.56.
7. 1980 c.44.
8. O.J. No. L216, 20.8.94, p.12.

PART II
RIGHTS AND OBLIGATIONS CONCERNING WORKING TIME

General

3. The provisions of this Part have effect subject to the exceptions provided for in Part III of these Regulations.

Maximum weekly working time

4. – (1) Subject to regulation 5, a worker's working time, including overtime, in any reference period which is applicable in his case shall not exceed an average of 48 hours for each seven days.

(2) An employer shall take all reasonable steps, in keeping with the need to protect the health and safety of workers, to ensure that the limit specified in paragraph (1) is complied with in the case of each worker employed by him in relation to whom it applies.

(3) Subject to paragraphs (4) and (5) and any agreement under regulation 23(b), the reference periods which apply in the case of a worker are –
   (a) where a relevant agreement provides for the application of this regulation in relation to successive periods of 17 weeks, each such period, or
   (b) in any other case, any period of 17 weeks in the course of his employment.

(4) Where a worker has worked for his employer for less than 17 weeks, the reference period applicable in his case is the period that has elapsed since he started work for his employer.

(5) Paragraphs (3) and (4) shall apply to a worker who is excluded from the scope of certain provisions of these Regulations by regulation 21 as if for each reference to 17 weeks there were substituted a reference to 26 weeks.

(6) For the purposes of this regulation, a worker's average working time for each seven days during a reference period shall be determined according to the formula –

$$\frac{(A + B)}{C}$$

where –
> **A**   is the aggregate number of hours comprised in the worker's working time during the course of the reference period;
>
> **B**   is the aggregate number of hours comprised in his working time during the course of the period beginning immediately after the end of the reference period and ending when the number of days in that subsequent period on which he has worked equals the number of excluded days during the reference period; and
>
> **C**   is the number of weeks in the reference period.

(7) In paragraph (6), 'excluded days' means days comprised in –
   (a) any period of annual leave taken by the worker in exercise of his entitlement under regulation 13;
   (b) any period of sick leave taken by the worker;
   (c) any period of maternity leave taken by the worker; and
   (d) any period in respect of which the limit specified in paragraph (1) did not apply in relation to the worker by virtue of regulation 5.

Agreement to exclude the maximum

5. – (1) The limit specified in regulation 4(1) shall not apply in relation to a worker who has agreed with his employer in writing that it should not apply in his case, provided that the employer complies with the requirements of paragraph (4).

(2) An agreement for the purposes of paragraph (1) –
   (a) may either relate to a specified period or apply indefinitely; and
   (b) subject to any provision in the agreement for a different period of notice, shall be terminable by the worker by giving not less than seven days' notice to his employer in writing.

(3) Where an agreement for the purposes of paragraph (1) makes provision for the termination of the agreement after a period of notice, the notice period provided for shall not exceed three months.

(4) The requirements referred to in paragraph (1) are that the employer –
   (a) maintains up-to-date records which –
      (i) identify each of the workers whom he employs who has agreed that the limit specified in regulation 4(1) should not apply in his case;
      (ii) set out any terms on which the worker agreed that the limit should not apply; and

      (iii)   specify the number of hours worked by him for the employer during each reference period since the agreement came into effect (excluding any period which ended more than two years before the most recent entry in the records);

    (b)   permits any inspector appointed by the Health and Safety Executive or any other authority which is responsible under regulation 28 for the enforcement of these Regulations to inspect those records on request; and

    (c)   provides any such inspector with such information as he may request regarding any case in which a worker has agreed that the limit specified in regulation 4(1) should not apply in his case.

Length of night work

6. – (1) A night worker's normal hours of work in any reference period which is applicable in his case shall not exceed an average of eight hours for each 24 hours.

(2) An employer shall take all reasonable steps, in keeping with the need to protect the health and safety of workers, to ensure that the limit specified in paragraph (1) is complied with in the case of each night worker employed by him.

(3) The reference periods which apply in the case of a night worker are –

    (a)   where a relevant agreement provides for the application of this regulation in relation to successive periods of 17 weeks, each such period, or

    (b)   in any other case, any period of 17 weeks in the course of his employment.

(4) Where a worker has worked for his employer for less than 17 weeks, the reference period applicable in his case is the period that has elapsed since he started work for his employer.

(5) For the purposes of this regulation, a night worker's average normal hours of work for each 24 hours during a reference period shall be determined according to the formula –

$$\frac{A}{(B - C)}$$

where –

A   is the number of hours during the reference period which are normal working hours for that worker;

B   is the number of days during the reference period, and

C   is the total number of hours during the reference period comprised in rest periods spent by the worker in pursuance of his entitlement under regulation 11, divided by 24.

(6) A night worker's normal hours of work for the purposes of this regulation are his normal working hours for the purposes of the 1996 Act in a case where section 234 of that Act (which provides for the interpretation of normal working hours in the case of certain employees) applies to him.

(7) An employer shall ensure that no night worker employed by him whose work involves special hazards or heavy physical or mental strain works for more than eight hours in any 24-hour period during which the night worker performs night work.

(8) For the purposes of paragraph (7), the work of a night worker shall be regarded as involving special hazards or heavy physical or mental strain if –

(a)   it is identified as such in –

(i)   a collective agreement, or

(ii)   a workforce agreement,
which takes account of the specific effects and hazards of night work, or

(b)   it is recognised in a risk assessment made by the employer under regulation 3 of the Management of Health and Safety at Work Regulations 1992[1] as involving a significant risk to the health or safety of workers employed by him.

Health assessment and transfer of night workers to day work

7. – (1) An employer –

(a)   shall not assign an adult worker to work which is to be undertaken during periods such that the worker will become a night worker unless –

(i)   the employer has ensured that the worker will have the opportunity of a free health assessment before he takes up the assignment; or

(ii)   the worker had a health assessment before being assigned to work to be undertaken during such periods on an earlier occasion, and the employer has no reason to believe that that assessment is no longer valid, and

(b)   shall ensure that each night worker employed by him has the opportunity of a free health assessment at regular intervals of whatever duration may be appropriate in his case.

(2) Subject to paragraph (4), an employer –
- (a)   shall not assign a young worker to work during the period between 10 pm and 6 am ('the restricted period') unless –
  - (i)   the employer has ensured that the young worker will have the opportunity of a free assessment of his health and capacities before he takes up the assignment; or
  - (ii)   the young worker had an assessment of his health and capacities before being assigned to work during the restricted period on an earlier occasion, and the employer has no reason to believe that that assessment is no longer valid; and
- (b)   shall ensure that each young worker employed by him and assigned to work during the restricted period has the opportunity of a free assessment of his health and capacities at regular intervals of whatever duration may be appropriate in his case.

(3)   For the purposes of paragraphs (1) and (2), an assessment is free if it is at no cost to the worker to whom it relates.

(4)   The requirements in paragraph (2) do not apply in a case where the work a young worker is assigned to do is of an exceptional nature.

(5)   No person shall disclose an assessment made for the purposes of this regulation to any person other than the worker to whom it relates, unless –
- (a)   the worker has given his consent in writing to the disclosure, or
- (b)   the disclosure is confined to a statement that the assessment shows the worker to be fit –
  - (i)   in a case where paragraph (1)(a)(i) or (2)(a)(i) applies, to take up an assignment, or
  - (ii)   in a case where paragraph (1)(b) or (2)(b) applies, to continue to undertake an assignment.

(6)   Where –
- (a)   a registered medical practitioner has advised an employer that a worker employed by the employer is suffering from health problems which the practitioner considers to be connected with the fact that the worker performs night work, and
- (b)   it is possible for the employer to transfer the worker to work –
  - (i)   to which the worker is suited, and
  - (ii)   which is to be undertaken during periods such that the worker will cease to be a night worker,
    the employer shall transfer the worker accordingly.

Pattern of work

8. Where the pattern according to which an employer organizes work is such as to put the health and safety of a worker employed by him at risk, in particular because the work is monotonous or the work-rate is predetermined, the employer shall ensure that the worker is given adequate rest breaks.

Records

9. An employer shall –
  (a) keep records which are adequate to show whether the limits specified in regulations 4(1) and 6(1) and (7) and the requirements in regulations 7(1) and (2) are being complied with in the case of each worker employed by him in relation to whom they apply; and
  (b) retain such records for two years from the date on which they were made.

Daily rest

10. – (1) An adult worker is entitled to a rest period of not less than eleven consecutive hours in each 24-hour period during which he works for his employer.

(2) Subject to paragraph (3), a young worker is entitled to a rest period of not less than twelve consecutive hours in each 24-hour period during which he works for his employer.

(3) The minimum rest period provided for in paragraph (2) may be interrupted in the case of activities involving periods of work that are split up over the day or of short duration.

Weekly rest period

11. – (1) Subject to paragraph (2), an adult worker is entitled to an uninterrupted rest period of not less than 24 hours in each seven-day period during which he works for his employer.

(2) If his employer so determines, an adult worker shall be entitled to either –

(a)   two uninterrupted rest periods each of not less than 24 hours in each 14-day period during which he works for his employer; or

(b)   one uninterrupted rest period of not less than 48 hours in each such 14-day period, in place of the entitlement provided for in paragraph (1).

(3) Subject to paragraph (8), a young worker is entitled to a rest period of not less than 48 hours in each seven-day period during which he works for his employer.

(4) For the purpose of paragraphs (1) to (3), a seven-day period or (as the case may be) 14-day period shall be taken to begin –

(a)   at such times on such days as may be provided for the purposes of this regulation in a relevant agreement; or

(b)   where there are no provisions of a relevant agreement which apply, at the start of each week or (as the case may be) every other week.

(5) In a case where, in accordance with paragraph (4), 14-day periods are to be taken to begin at the start of every other week, the first such period applicable in the case of a particular worker shall be taken to begin –

(a)   if the worker's employment began on or before the date on which these Regulations come into force, on 5th October 1998; or

(b)   if the worker's employment begins after the date on which these Regulations come into force, at the start of the week in which that employment begins.

(6) For the purposes of paragraphs (4) and (5), a week starts at midnight between Sunday and Monday.

(7) The minimum rest period to which an adult worker is entitled under paragraph (1) or (2) shall not include any part of a rest period to which the worker is entitled under regulation 10(1), except where this is justified by objective or technical reasons or reasons concerning the organization of work.

(8) The minimum rest period to which a young worker is entitled under paragraph (3) –

(a)   may be interrupted in the case of activities involving periods of work that are split up over the day or are of short duration; and

(b)   may be reduced where this is justified by technical or organization reasons, but not to less than 36 consecutive hours.

Rest breaks

12. – (1) Where an adult worker's daily working time is more than six hours, he is entitled to a rest break.

(2) The details of the rest break to which an adult worker is entitled under paragraph (1), including its duration and the terms on which it is granted, shall be in accordance with any provisions for the purposes of this regulation which are contained in a collective agreement or a workforce agreement.

(3) Subject to the provisions of any applicable collective agreement or workforce agreement, the rest break provided for in paragraph (1) is an uninterrupted period of not less than 20 minutes, and the worker is entitled to spend it away from his workstation if he has one.

(4) Where a young worker's daily working time is more than four and a half hours, he is entitled to a rest break of at least 30 minutes, which shall be consecutive if possible, and he is entitled to spend it away from his workstation if he has one.

(5) If, on any day, a young worker is employed by more than one employer, his daily working time shall be determined for the purpose of paragraph (4) by aggregating the number of hours worked by him for each employer.

Entitlement to annual leave

13. – (1) Subject to paragraphs (5) and (7), a worker is entitled in each leave year to a period of leave determined in accordance with paragraph (2).

(2) The period of leave to which a worker is entitled under paragraph (1) is –
- (a) in any leave year beginning on or before 23rd November 1998, three weeks;
- (b) in any leave year beginning after 23rd November 1998 but before 23rd November 1999, three weeks and a proportion of a fourth week equivalent to the proportion of the year beginning on 23rd November 1998 which has elapsed at the start of that leave year; and
- (c) in any leave year beginning after 23rd November 1999, four weeks.

(3) A worker's leave year, for the purposes of this regulation, begins –

    (a)   on such date during the calendar year as may be provided for in a relevant agreement; or

    (b)   where there are no provisions of a relevant agreement which apply –

      (i)   if the worker's employment began on or before 1st October 1998, on that date and each subsequent anniversary of that date; or

      (ii)   if the worker's employment begins after 1st October 1998, on the date on which that employment begins and each subsequent anniversary of that date.

(4) Paragraph (3) does not apply to a worker to whom Schedule 2 applies (workers employed in agriculture) except where, in the case of a worker partly employed in agriculture, a relevant agreement so provides.

(5) Where the date on which a worker's employment begins is later than the date on which (by virtue of a relevant agreement) his first leave year begins, the leave to which he is entitled in that leave year is a proportion of the period applicable under paragraph (2) equal to the proportion of that leave year remaining on the date on which his employment begins.

(6) Where by virtue of paragraph (2)(b) or (5) the period of leave to which a worker is entitled is or includes a proportion of a week, the proportion shall be determined in days and any fraction of a day shall be treated as a whole day.

(7) The entitlement conferred by paragraph (1) does not arise until a worker has been continuously employed for thirteen weeks.

(8) For the purposes of paragraph (7), a worker has been continuously employed for thirteen weeks if his relations with his employer have been governed by a contract during the whole or part of each of those weeks.

(9) Leave to which a worker is entitled under this regulation may be taken in instalments, but –

    (a)   it may only be taken in the leave year in respect of which it is due, and

    (b)   it may not be replaced by a payment in lieu except where the worker's employment is terminated.

Compensation related to entitlement to leave

14. – (1) This regulation applies where –

(a)   a worker's employment is terminated during the course of his leave year, and

(b)   on the date on which the termination takes effect ('the termination date'), the proportion he has taken of the leave to which he is entitled in the leave year under regulation 13(1) differs from the proportion of the leave year which has expired.

(2)   Where the proportion of leave taken by the worker is less than the proportion of the leave year which has expired, his employer shall make him a payment in lieu of leave in accordance with paragraph (3).

(3)   The payment due under paragraph (2) shall be –

(a)   such sum as may be provided for the purposes of this regulation in a relevant agreement, or

(b)   where there are no provisions of a relevant agreement which apply, a sum equal to the amount that would be due to the worker under regulation 16 in respect of a period of leave determined according to the formula –

$$(A \times B) - C$$

where –

A   is the period of leave to which the worker is entitled under regulation 13(1);

B   is the proportion of the worker's leave year which expired before the termination date, and

C   is the period of leave taken by the worker between the start of the leave year and the termination date.

(4)   A relevant agreement may provide that, where the proportion of leave taken by the worker exceeds the proportion of the leave year which has expired, he shall compensate his employer, whether by a payment, by undertaking additional work or otherwise.

Dates on which leave is taken

15. – (1) A worker may take leave to which he is entitled under regulation 13(1) on such days as he may elect by giving notice to his employer in accordance with paragraph (3), subject to any requirement imposed on him by his employer under paragraph (2).

(2)   A worker's employer may require the worker –

(a)   to take leave to which the worker is entitled under regulation 13(1); or

(b)   not to take such leave,

on particular days, by giving notice to the worker in accordance with paragraph (3).

(3) A notice under paragraph (1) or (2) –
  (a) may relate to all or part of the leave to which a worker is entitled in a leave year;
  (b) shall specify the days on which leave is or (as the case may be) is not to be taken and, where the leave on a particular day is to be in respect of only part of the day, its duration; and
  (c) shall be given to the employer or, as the case may be, the worker before the relevant date.

(4) The relevant date, for the purposes of paragraph (3), is the date –
  (a) in the case of a notice under paragraph (1) or (2)(a), twice as many days in advance of the earliest day specified in the notice as the number of days or part-days to which the notice relates, and
  (b) in the case of a notice under paragraph (2)(b), as many days in advance of the earliest day so specified as the number of days or part-days to which the notice relates.

(5) Any right or obligation under paragraphs (1) to (4) may be varied or excluded by a relevant agreement.

(6) This regulation does not apply to a worker to whom Schedule 2 applies (workers employed in agriculture) except where, in the case of a worker partly employed in agriculture, a relevant agreement so provides.

Payment in respect of periods of leave

16. – (1) A worker is entitled to be paid in respect of any period of annual leave to which he is entitled under regulation 13, at the rate of a week's pay in respect of each week of leave.

(2) Sections 221 to 224 of the 1996 Act shall apply for the purpose of determining the amount of a week's pay for the purposes of this regulation, subject to the modifications set out in paragraph (3).

(3) The provisions referred to in paragraph (2) shall apply –
  (a) as if references to the employee were references to the worker;
  (b) as if references to the employee's contract of employment were references to the worker's contract;
  (c) as if the calculation date were the first day of the period of leave in question; and

(d)   as if the references to sections 227 and 228 did not apply.

(4) A right to payment under paragraph (1) does not affect any right of a worker to remuneration under his contract ('contractual remuneration').

(5) Any contractual remuneration paid to a worker in respect of a period of leave goes towards discharging any liability of the employer to make payments under this regulation in respect of that period; and, conversely, any payment of remuneration under this regulation in respect of a period goes towards discharging any liability of the employer to pay contractual remuneration in respect of that period.

Entitlements under other provisions

17. Where during any period a worker is entitled to a rest period, rest break or annual leave both under a provision of these Regulations and under a separate provision (including a provision of his contract), he may not exercise the two rights separately, but may, in taking a rest period, break or leave during that period, take advantage of whichever right is, in any particular respect, the more favourable.

---

1. SI 1992/2051, amended by SI 1994/2865 and 1997/135.

PART III
EXCEPTIONS

Excluded sectors

18. Regulations 4(1) and (2), 6(1), (2) and (7), 7(1), and (6), 8, 10(1), 11(1) and (2), 12(1), 13 and 16 do not apply –

(a)   to the following sectors of activity –
  (i)   air, rail, road, sea, inland waterway and lake transport;
  (ii)   sea fishing;
  (iii)   other work at sea; or
(b)   to the activities of doctors in training, or
(c)   where characteristics peculiar to certain specified services such as the armed forces or the police, or to certain specific activities in the civil protection services, inevitably conflict with the provisions of these Regulations.

Domestic service

19. Regulations 4(1) and (2), 6(1), (2) and (7), 7(1), (2) and (6) and 8 do not apply in relation to a worker employed as a domestic servant in a private household.

Unmeasured working time

20. Regulations 4(1) and (2), 6(1), (2) and (7), 10(1), 11(1) and (2) and 12(1) do not apply in relation to a worker where, on account of the specific characteristics of the activity in which he is engaged, the duration of his working time is not measured or predetermined or can be determined by the worker himself, as may be the case for –

(a)   managing executives or other persons with autonomous decision-taking powers;
(b)   family workers; or
(c)   workers officiating at religious ceremonies in churches and religious communities.

Other special cases

21. Subject to regulation 24, regulations 6(1), (2) and (7), 10(1), 11(1) and (2) and 12(1) do not apply in relation to a worker –

(a)   where the worker's activities are such that his place of work and place of residence are distant from one another or his different places of work are distant from one another;

(b)   where the worker is engaged in security and surveillance activities requiring a permanent presence in order to protect property and persons, as may be the case for security guards and caretakers or security firms;

(c)   where the worker's activities involve the need for continuity of service or production, as may be the case in relation to –

  (i)   services relating to the reception, treatment or care provided by hospitals or similar establishments, residential institutions and prisons;

  (ii)   work at docks or airports;

  (iii) press, radio, television, cinematographic production, postal and telecommunications services and civil protection services;

  (iv) gas, water and electricity production, transmission and distribution, household refuse collection and incineration;

  (v)   industries in which work cannot be interrupted on technical grounds;

  (vi) research and development activities;

  (vii) agriculture;

(d)   where there is a foreseeable surge of activity, as may be the case in relation to –

  (i)   agriculture;

  (ii)   tourism; and

  (iii) postal services;

(e)   where the worker's activities are affected by –

  (i)   an occurrence due to unusual and unforeseeable circumstances, beyond the control of the worker's employer;

  (ii)   exceptional events, the consequences of which could not have been avoided despite the exercise of all due care by the employer; or

  (iii) an accident or the imminent risk of an accident.

Shift workers

22. – (1) Subject to regulation 24 –

(a)   regulation 10(1) does not apply in relation to a shift worker when he changes shift and cannot take a daily rest period between the end of one shift and the start of the next one;

(b)   paragraphs (1) and (2) of regulation 11 do not apply in relation to a shift worker when he changes shift and cannot take a weekly rest period between the end of one shift and the start of the next one; and

(c)   neither regulation 10(1) nor paragraphs (1) and (2) of regulation

11 apply to workers engaged in activities involving periods of work split up over the day, as may be the case for cleaning staff.

(2) For the purposes of this regulation –
'shift worker' means any worker whose work schedule is part of shift work; and
'shift work' means any method of organizing work in shifts whereby workers succeed each other at the same workstations according to a certain pattern, including a rotating pattern, and which may be continuous or discontinuous, entailing the need for workers to work at different times over a given period of days or weeks.

Collective and workforce agreements

23. A collective agreement or a workforce agreement may –
    (a)   modify or exclude the application of regulations 6(1) to (3) and (7), 10(1), 11(1) and (2) and 12(1), and
    (b)   for objective or technical reasons or reasons concerning the organization of work, modify the application of regulation 4(3) and (4) by the substitution, for each reference to 17 weeks, of a different period, being a period not exceeding 52 weeks,
in relation to particular workers or groups of workers.

Compensatory rest

24. Where the application of any provision of these Regulations is excluded by regulation 21 or 22, or is modified or excluded by means of a collective agreement or a workforce agreement under regulation 23(a), and a worker is accordingly required by his employer to work during a period which would otherwise be a rest period or rest break –
    (a)   his employer shall wherever possible allow him to take an equivalent period of compensatory rest, and
    (b)   in exceptional cases in which it is not possible, for objective reasons, to grant such a period of rest, his employer shall afford him such protection as may be appropriate in order to safeguard the worker's health and safety.

Workers in the armed forces

25. (1) Regulation 9 does not apply in relation to a worker serving as a member of the armed forces.

(2) Regulations 10(2) and 11(3) do not apply in relation to a young worker serving as a member of the armed forces.

(3) In a case where a young worker is accordingly required to work during a period which would otherwise be a rest period, he shall be allowed an appropriate period of compensatory rest.

Young workers employed on ships

26. Regulations 7(2), 10(2), 11(3) and 12(4) do not apply in relation to a young worker whose employment is subject to regulation under section 55(2)(b) of the Merchant Shipping Act 1995[1].

Young workers: force majeure

27. – (1) Regulations 10(2) and 12(4) do not apply in relation to a young worker where his employer requires him to undertake work which no adult worker is available to perform and which –
    (a)   is occasioned by either –
      (i)   an occurrence due to unusual and unforseeable circumstances, beyond the employer's control, or
      (ii)   exceptional events, the consequences of which could not have been avoided despite the exercise of all due care by the employer;
    (b)   is of a temporary nature; and
    (c)   must be performed immediately.

(2) Where the application of regulation 10(2) or 12(4) is excluded by paragraph (1), and a young worker is accordingly required to work during a period which would otherwise be a rest period or rest break, his employer shall allow him to take an equivalent period of compensatory rest within the following three weeks.

---

1. 1995 c.21.

PART IV
MISCELLANEOUS

Enforcement

28. – (1) In this regulation and regulation 29 –
'the 1974 Act' means the Health and Safety at Work etc Act 1974[1];
'the relevant requirements' means the following provisions –
  (a) regulations 4(2), 6(2) and (7), 7(1), (2) and (6), 8 and 9; and
  (b) regulation 24, in so far as it applies where regulation 6(1), (2) or (7) is modified or excluded, and
'the relevant statutory provisions' has the same meaning as in the 1974 Act.

(2) It shall be the duty of the Health and Safety Executive to make adequate arrangements for the enforcement of the relevant requirements except to the extent that a local authority is made responsible for their enforcement by paragraph (3).

(3) Where the relevant requirements apply in relation to workers employed in premises in respect of which a local authority is responsible, under the Health and Safety (Enforcing Authority) Regulations 1998[2], for enforcing any of the relevant statutory provisions, it shall be the duty of that authority to enforce those requirements.

(4) The duty imposed on local authorities by paragraph (3) shall be performed in accordance with such guidance as may be given to them by the Health and Safety Commission.

(5) The following provisions of the 1974 Act shall apply in relation to the enforcement of the relevant requirements as they apply in relation to the enforcement of the relevant statutory provisions, and as if any reference in those provisions to an enforcing authority were a reference to the Health and Safety Executive and any local authority made responsible for the enforcement of the relevant requirements –
  (a) section 19;
  (b) section 20(1), (2)(a) to (d) and (j) to (m), (7) and (8); and
  (c) sections 21, 22[3], 23(1), (2) and (5), 24 and 26; and
  (d) section 28, in so far as it relates to information obtained by an inspector in pursuance of a requirement imposed under section 22(2)(j) or (k).

(6) Any function of the Health and Safety Commission under the 1974 Act which is exercisable in relation to the enforcement by the Health and

Safety Executive of the relevant statutory provisions shall be exercisable in relation to the enforcement by the Executive of the relevant requirements.

Offences

29. – (1) An employer who fails to comply with any of the relevant requirements shall be guilty of an offence.

(2) The following provisions of section 33(1) of the 1974 Act shall apply where an inspector is exercising or has exercised any power conferred by a provision specified in regulation 28(5) –
   (a)   paragraph (e), in so far as it refers to section 20;
   (b)   paragraphs (f) and (g);
   (c)   paragraph (h), in so far as it refers to an inspector;
   (d)   paragraph (j) in so far as it refers to section 28; and
   (e)   paragraph (k).

(3) An employer guilty of an offence under paragraph (1) shall be liable –
   (a)   on summary conviction, to a fine not exceeding the statutory maximum;
   (b)   on conviction on indictment, to a fine.

(4) A person guilty of an offence under a provision of section 33(1) of the 1974 Act as applied by paragraph (2) shall be liable to the penalty prescribed in relation to that provision by subsection (2), (2A) or (3) of section 33[4], as the case may be.

(5) Sections 36(1), 37 to 39 and 42(1) to (3) of the 1974 Act shall apply in relation to the offences provided for in paragraphs (1) and (2) as they apply in relation to offences under the relevant statutory provisions.

Remedies

30. – (1) A worker may present a complaint to an employment tribunal that his employer –
   (a)   has refused to permit him to exercise any right he has under –
   (i)   regulation 10(1) or (2), 11(1), (2) or (3), 12(1) or (4) or 13(1);
   (ii)   regulation 24, in so far as it applies where regulation 10(1), 11(1) or (2) or 12(1) is modified or excluded; or
   (iii) regulation 25(3) or 27(2); or
   (b)   has failed to pay him the whole or any part of any amount due to him under regulation 14(2) or 16(1).

(2) An employment tribunal shall not consider a complaint under this regulation unless it is presented –

    (a)   before the end of the period of three months (or, in a case to which regulation 38(2) applies, six months) beginning with the date on which it is alleged that the exercise of the right should have been permitted (or in the case of a rest period or leave extending over more than one day, the date on which it should have been permitted to begin) or, as the case may be, the payment should have been made;

    (b)   within such further period as the tribunal considers reasonable in a case where it is satisfied that it was not reasonably practicable for the complaint to be presented before the end of that period of three or, as the case may be, six months.

(3) Where an employment tribunal finds a complaint under paragraph (1)(a) well-founded, the tribunal –

    (a)   shall make a declaration to that effect, and

    (b)   may make an award of compensation to be paid by the employer to the worker.

(4) The amount of the compensation shall be such as the tribunal considers just and equitable in all the circumstances having regard to –

    (a)   the employer's default in refusing to permit the worker to exercise his right, and

    (b)   any loss sustained by the worker which is attributable to the matters complained of.

(5) Where on a complaint under paragraph (1)(b) an employment tribunal finds that an employer has failed to pay a worker in accordance with regulation 14(2) or 16(1), it shall order the employer to pay to the worker the amount which it finds to be due to him.

Right not to suffer detriment

31. – (1) After section 45 of the 1996 Act there shall be inserted –

Working time cases '**45A.** – (1) A worker has the right not to be subjected to any detriment by any act, or any deliberate failure to act, by his employer done on the ground that the worker –

    (a)   refused (or proposed to refuse) to comply with a requirement which the employer imposed (or proposed to impose) in contravention of the Working Time Regulations 1998,

    (b)   refused (or proposed to refuse) to forgo a right conferred on him by those Regulations,

    (c)   failed to sign a workforce agreement for the purposes of those Regulations, or to enter into, or agree to vary or extend, any other agreement with his employer which is provided for in those Regulations,

    (d)   being –

        (i)   a representative of members of the workforce for the purposes of Schedule 1 to those Regulations, or

        (ii)   a candidate in an election in which any person elected will, on being elected, be such a representative,

    performed (or proposed to perform) any functions or activities as such a representative or candidate,

    (e)   brought proceedings against the employer to enforce a right conferred on him by those Regulations, or

    (f)   alleged that the employer had infringed such a right.

(2) It is immaterial for the purposes of subsection (1)(e) or (f) –

    (a)   whether or not the worker has the right, or

    (b)   whether or not the right has been infringed,

but, for those provisions to apply, the claim to the right and that it has been infringed must be made in good faith.

(3)   It is sufficient for subsection (1)(f) to apply that the worker, without specifying the right, made it reasonably clear to the employer what the right claimed to have been infringed was.

(4)   This section does not apply where a worker is an employee and the detriment in question amounts to dismissal within the meaning of Part X, unless the dismissal is in circumstances in which, by virtue of section 197, Part X does not apply.'

(2) After section 48(1) of the 1996 Act there shall be inserted the following subsection –

'(1ZA)A worker may present a complaint to an employment tribunal that he has been subjected to a detriment in contravention of section 45A.'

(3) In section 49 of the 1996 Act[5] (remedies) –
   (a)   in subsection (2), for 'subsection (6)' there shall be substituted 'subsections (5A) and (6)', and
   (b)   after subsection (5), there shall be inserted –
   '(5A) Where –
      (a)   the complaint is made under section 48 (1ZA),
      (b)   the detriment to which the worker is subjected is the termination of his worker's contract, and
      (c)   that contract is not a contract of employment,
   any compensation must not exceed the compensation that would be payable under Chapter II of Part X if the worker had been an employee and had been dismissed for the reason specified in section 101A.'

(4) In section 192(2) of the 1996 Act (provisions applicable in relation to service in the armed forces), after paragraph (a) there shall be inserted –
   '(aa) in Part V, section 45A, and sections 48 and 49 so far as relating to that section,'

(5) In sections 194(2)(c), 195(2)(c) and 202(2)(b) of the 1996 Act, for 'sections 44 and 47' there shall be substituted 'sections 44, 45A and 47'.

(6) In section 200(1) of the 1996 Act (which lists provisions of the Act which do not apply to employment in police service), after '45,' there shall be inserted '45A,'.

(7) In section 205 of the 1996 Act (remedy for infringement of certain rights), after subsection (1) there shall be inserted the following subsection –
   '(1ZA)In relation to the right conferred by section 45A, the reference in subsection (1) to an employee has effect as a reference to a worker.'

Unfair dismissal

32. – (1) After section 101 of the 1996 Act there shall be inserted the following section –
'Working time cases   **101A.** An employee who is dismissed shall be regarded for the purposes of this Part as unfairly

dismissed if the reason (or, if more than one, the principal reason) for the dismissal is that the employee –

(a) refused (or proposed to refuse) to comply with a requirement which the employer imposed (or proposed to impose) in contravention of the Working Time Regulations 1998,

SI 1998/1833

(b) refused (or proposed to refuse) to forgo a right conferred on him by those Regulations,

(c) failed to sign a workforce agreement for the purposes of those Regulations, or to enter into, or agree to vary or extend, any other agreement with his employer which is provided for in those Regulations, or

(d) being –

   (i) a representative of members of the workforce for the purposes of Schedule 1 to those Regulations, or

   (ii) a candidate in an election in which any person elected will, on being elected, be such a representative,

performed (or proposed to perform) any functions or activities as such a representative or candidate.'

(2) In section 104 of the 1996 Act (right of employees not to be unfairly dismissed for asserting particular rights) in subsection (4) –

(a) at the end of paragraph (b), the word 'and' shall be omitted, and

(b) after paragraph (c), there shall be inserted the words –
   'and
   (d) the rights conferred by the Working Time

SI 1998/1833   Regulations 1998.'

(3) In section 105 of the 1996 Act (redundancy as unfair dismissal), after subsection (4) there shall be inserted the following subsection –
   '(4A) This subsection applies if the reason (or, if more than one, the principal reason) for which the employee was selected for dismissal was one of those specified in section 101A.'

(4) In sections 108(3) and 109(2) of the 1996 Act, after paragraph (d) there shall be inserted –
   '(dd) section 101A applies,'

203

(5) In sections 117(4)(b), 118(3), 120(1), 122(3), 128(1)(b) and 129(1) of the 1996 Act, after '100(1)(a) and (b),' there shall be inserted '101A(d),'.

(6) In section 202(2) (cases where disclosure of information is restricted on ground of national security) –

    (a)   in paragraph (g)(i), after '100' there shall be inserted ', 101A(d)', and

    (b)   in paragraph (g)(ii), after 'of that section,' there shall be inserted 'or by reason of the application of subsection (4A) in so far as it applies where the reason (or, if more than one, the principal reason) for which an employee was selected for dismissal was that specified in section 101A(d)'.

(7) In section 209(2) of the 1996 Act (which lists provisions excluded from the scope of the power to amend the Act by order), after '101,' in paragraph (e) there shall be inserted '101A,'.

(8) In sections 237(1A) and 238(2A) of the Trade Union and Labour Relations (Consolidation) Act 1992[6] (cases where employee can complain of unfair dismissal notwithstanding industrial action at time of dismissal), after '100' there shall be inserted ', 101A(d)'.

(9) In section 10(5)(a) of the Employment Tribunals Act 1996 (cases where Minister's certificate is not conclusive evidence that action was taken to safeguard national security), after '100' there shall be inserted ', 101A(d)'.

Conciliation

33. In section 18(1) of the Employment Tribunals Act 1996[7] (cases where conciliation provisions apply) –

    (a)   at the end of paragraph (e), the word 'or' shall be omitted, and

    (b)   after paragraph (f), there shall be inserted the words

SI 1998/1833   'or

        (ff) under regulation 30 of the Working Time Regulations 1998,'.

Appeals

34. In section 21 of the Employment Tribunals Act 1996 (jurisdiction of the Employment Appeal Tribunal) –

    (a)   at the end of subsection (1) (which confers jurisdiction by reference to Acts under or by virtue of which decisions are made) there shall be inserted –

SI 1998/1833   'or under the Working Time Regulations 1998.';

(b)   in subsection (2), after 'the Acts listed' there shall be inserted –
'or the Regulations referred to'.

Restrictions on contracting out

35. – (1) Any provision in an agreement (whether a contract of employment or not) is void in so far as it purports –
(a)   to exclude or limit the operation of any provision of these Regulations, save in so far as these Regulations provide for an agreement to have that effect, or
(b)   to preclude a person from bringing proceedings under these Regulations before an employment tribunal.

(2)   Paragraph (1) does not apply to –
(a)   any agreement to refrain from instituting or continuing proceedings where a conciliation officer has taken action under section 18 of the Employment Tribunals Act 1996 (conciliation); or
(b)   any agreement to refrain from instituting or continuing proceedings within section 18(1)(ff) of the Employment Tribunals Act 1996 (proceedings under these Regulations where conciliation is available), if the conditions regulating compromise agreements under these Regulations are satisfied in relation to the agreement.

(3)   For the purposes of paragraph (2)(b) the conditions regulating compromise agreements under these Regulations arc that –
(a)   the agreement must be in writing,
(b)   the agreement must relate to the particular complaint,
(c)   the worker must have received advice from a relevant independent adviser as to the terms and effect of the proposed agreement and, in particular, its effect on his ability to pursue his rights before an employment tribunal,
(d)   there must be in force, when the adviser gives the advice, a contract of insurance, or an indemnity provided for members of a profession or professional body, covering the risk of a claim by the worker in respect of loss arising in consequence of the advice,
(e)   the agreement must identify the adviser, and
(f)   the agreement must state that the conditions regulating compromise agreements under these Regulations are satisfied.

(4)   A person is a relevant independent adviser for the purposes of paragraph (3)(c) –
(a)   if he is a qualified lawyer,

(b)   if he is an officer, official, employee or member of an independent trade union who has been certified in writing by the trade union as competent to give advice and as authorised to do so on behalf of the trade union, or

(c)   if he works at an advice centre (whether as an employee or as a volunteer) and has been certified in writing by the centre as competent to give advice and as authorised to do so on behalf of the centre.

(5) But a person is not a relevant independent adviser for the purposes of paragraph (3)(c) in relation to the worker –

(a)   if he, is employed by or is acting in the matter for the employer or an associated employer,

(b)   in the case of a person within paragraph (4)(b) or (c), if the trade union or advice centre is the employer or an associated employer, or

(c)   in the case of a person within paragraph (4)(c), if the worker makes a payment for the advice received from him.

(6) In paragraph (4)(a), 'qualified lawyer' means –

(a)   as respects England and Wales, a barrister (whether in practice as such or employed to give legal advice), a solicitor who holds a practising certificate, or a person other than a barrister or solicitor who is an authorised advocate or authorised litigator (within the meaning of the Courts and Legal Services Act 1990)[8]; and

(b)   as respects Scotland, an advocate (whether in practice as such or employed to give legal advice), or a solicitor who holds a practising certificate.

(7) For the purposes of paragraph (5) any two employers shall be treated as associated if –

(a)   one is a company of which the other (directly or indirectly) has control; or

(b)   both are companies of which a third person (directly or indirectly) has control; and 'associated employer' shall be construed accordingly.

---

1. 1974 c.37.

2. SI 1998/494.

3. Section 22 of the 1974 Act was amended by the Consumer Protection Act 1987 (c.43), Schedule 3, paragraph 2.

4. Subsection (2A) of section 33 of the 1974 Act was inserted by the Offshore Safety Act 1992 (c.15), section 4(3).

5. Section 49 of the 1996 Act was amended by the Public Interest Disclosure Act 1998 (c. 23) section 4.

6. 1992 c.52: subsection (1A) of section 237 and subsection (2A) of section 238 were inserted by the Trade Union Reform and Employment Rights Act 1993 (c.19), Schedule 8, paragraphs 76 and 77.

7. 1996 c.17; section 1(2) of the Employment Rights (Dispute Resolution) Act 1998 (c.8) provides for the Industrial Tribunals Act 1996 to be cited as the Employment Tribunals Act 1996.

8. 1990 c.41.

PART V

Special Classes of Person

Agency workers not otherwise 'workers'

36. – (1) This regulation applies in any case where an individual ('the agency worker') –

    (a)   is supplied by a person ('the agent') to do work for another ('the principal') under a contract or other arrangements made between the agent and the principal; but

    (b)   is not, as respects that work, a worker, because of the absence of a worker's contract between the individual and the agent or the principal; and

    (c)   is not a party to a contract under which he undertakes to do the work for another party to the contract whose status is, by virtue of the contract, that of a client or customer of any profession or business undertaking carried on by the individual.

(2) In a case where this regulation applies, the other provisions of these Regulations shall have effect as if there were a worker's contract for the doing of the work by the agency worker made between the agency worker and –

    (a)   whichever of the agent and the principal is responsible for paying the agency worker in respect of the work; or

    (b)   if neither the agent nor the principal is so responsible, whichever of them pays the agency worker in respect of the work,

and as if that person were the agency worker's employer.

Crown employment

37. – (1) Subject to paragraph (4) and regulation 38, these Regulations have effect in relation to Crown employment and persons in Crown employment as they have effect in relation to other employment and other workers.

(2) In paragraph (1) 'Crown employment' means employment under or for the purposes of a government department or any officer or body exercising on behalf of the Crown functions conferred by a statutory provision.

(3) For the purposes of the application of the provisions of these Regulations in relation to Crown employment in accordance with paragraph (1) –

(a)   references to a worker shall be construed as references to a person in Crown employment; and

(b)   references to a worker's contract shall be construed as references to the terms of employment of a person in Crown employment.

(4) No act or omission by the Crown which is an offence under regulation 29 shall make the Crown criminally liable, but the High Court or, in Scotland, the Court of Session may, on the application of a person appearing to the Court to have an interest, declare any such act or omission unlawful.

Armed forces

38. – (1) Regulation 37 applies –

(a)   subject to paragraph (2), to service as a member of the armed forces, and

(b)   to employment by an association established for the purposes of Part XI of the Reserve Forces Act 1996.[1]

(2) No complaint concerning the service of any person as a member of the armed forces may be presented to an employment tribunal under regulation 30 unless –

(a)   that person has made a complaint in respect of the same matter to an officer under the service redress procedures, and

(b)   that complaint has not been withdrawn.

(3) For the purpose of paragraph (2)(b), a person shall be treated as having withdrawn his complaint if, having made a complaint to an officer under the service redress procedures, he fails to submit the complaint to the Defence Council under those procedures.

(4) Where a complaint of the kind referred to in paragraph (2) is presented to an employment tribunal, the service redress procedures may continue after the complaint is presented.

(5) In this regulation, 'the service redress procedures' means the procedures, excluding those which relate to the making of a report on a complaint to Her Majesty, referred to in section 180 of the Army Act 1955,[2] section 180 of the Air Force Act 1955[3] and section 130 of the Naval Discipline Act 1957.[4,5]

House of Lords staff

39. – (1) These Regulations have effect in relation to employment as a relevant member of the House of Lords staff as they have effect in relation to other employment.

(2) Nothing in any rule of law or the law or practice of Parliament prevents a relevant member of the House of Lords staff from presenting a complaint to an employment tribunal under regulation 30.

(3) In this regulation 'relevant member of the House of Lords staff' means any person who is employed under a worker's contract with the Corporate Officer of the House of Lords.

House of Commons staff

40. – (1) These Regulations have effect in relation to employment as a relevant member of the House of Commons staff as they have effect in relation to other employment.

(2) For the purposes of the application of the provisions of these Regulations in relation to a relevant member of the House of Commons staff –

(a) references to a worker shall be construed as references to a relevant member of the House of Commons staff; and

(b) references to a worker's contract shall be construed as references to the terms of employment of a relevant member of the House of Commons staff.

(3) Nothing in any rule of law or the law or practice of Parliament prevents a relevant member of the House of Commons staff from presenting a complaint to an employment tribunal under regulation 30.

(4) In this regulation 'relevant member of the House of Commons staff' means any person –

(a) who was appointed by the House of Commons Commission; or

(b) who is a member of the Speaker's personal staff.

Police service

41. – (1) For the purposes of these Regulations, the holding, otherwise than under a contract of employment, of the office of constable or an appointment as a police cadet shall be treated as employment, under a worker's contract, by the relevant officer.

(2) Any matter relating to the employment of a worker which may be provided for the purposes of these Regulations in a workforce agreement may be provided for the same purposes in relation to the service of a person holding the office of constable or an appointment as a police cadet by an agreement between the relevant officer and a joint branch board.

(3) In this regulation –
'a joint branch board' means a joint branch board constituted in accordance with regulation 7(3) of the Police Federation Regulations 1969[6] or regulation 7(3) of the Police Federation (Scotland) Regulations 1985[7], and
'the relevant officer' means –

   (a)   in relation to a member of a police force or a special constable or police cadet appointed for a police area, the chief officer of police (or, in Scotland, the chief constable);

   (b)   in relation to a person holding office under section 9(1)(b) or 55(1)(b) of the Police Act 1997[8] (police members of the National Criminal Intelligence Service and the National Crime Squad), the Director General of the National Criminal Intelligence Service or, as the case may be, the Director General of the National Crime Squad; and

   (c)   in relation to any other person holding the office of constable or an appointment as a police cadet, the person who has the direction and control of the body of constables or cadets in question.

Non-employed trainees

42. For the purposes of these Regulations, a person receiving relevant training, otherwise than under a contract of employment, shall be regarded as a worker, and the person whose undertaking is providing the training shall be regarded as his employer.

Agricultural workers

43. The provisions of Schedule 2 have effect in relation to workers employed in agriculture.

Ian McCartney
Minister of State,
Department of Trade and Industry

30th July 1998

1. 1996 c.14.
2. 1955 c.18.
3. 1955 c.19.
4. 1957 c.53.
5. Each of the sections referred to in paragraph (5) was substituted by section 20 of the Armed Forces Act 1996 (c.46).
6. SI 1969/1787, to which there are amendments not relevant to these Regulations.
7. SI 1985/1531, to which there are amendments not relevant to these Regulations.
8. 1997 c.16.

SCHEDULE 1

WORKFORCE AGREEMENTS

1. An agreement is a workforce agreement for the purposes of these Regulations if the following conditions are satisfied –

(a)   the agreement is in writing;

(b)   it has effect for a specified period not exceeding five years;

(c)   it applies either –

    (i)   to all of the relevant members of the workforce, or

    (ii)   to all of the relevant members of the workforce who belong to a particular group;

(d)   the agreement is signed –

    (i)   in the case of an agreement of the kind referred to in sub-paragraph (c)(i), by the representatives of the workforce, and in the case of an agreement of the kind referred to in sub-paragraph (c)(ii) by the representatives of the group to which the agreement applies (excluding, in either case, any representative not a relevant member of the workforce on the date on which the agreement was first made available for signature), or

    (ii)   if the employer employed 20 or fewer workers on the date referred to in sub-paragraph (d)(i), either by the appropriate representatives in accordance with that sub-paragraph or by the majority of the workers employed by him;

(e)   before the agreement was made available for signature, the employer provided all the workers to whom it was intended to apply on the date on which it came into effect with copies of the text of the agreement and such guidance as those workers might reasonably require in order to understand it fully.

2. For the purposes of this Schedule –

'a particular group' is a group of the relevant members of a workforce who undertake a particular function, work at a particular workplace or belong to a particular department or unit within their employer's business;

'relevant members of the workforce' are all of the workers employed by a particular employer, excluding any worker whose terms and conditions of employment are provided for, wholly or in part, in a collective agreement;

'representatives of the workforce' are workers duly elected to represent the relevant members of the workforce, 'representatives of the group' are workers duly elected to represent the members of a particular group, and representatives are 'duly elected' if the election at which they were elected satisfied the requirements of paragraph 3 of this Schedule.

3. The requirements concerning elections referred to in paragraph 2 are that –

(a)   the number of representatives to be elected is determined by the employer;

(b)   the candidates for election as representatives of the workforce are relevant members of the workforce, and the candidates for election as representatives of a group are members of the group;

(c)   no worker who is eligible to be a candidate is unreasonably excluded from standing for election;

(d)   all the relevant members of the workforce are entitled to vote for representatives of the workforce, and all the members of a particular group are entitled to vote for representatives of the group;

(e)   the workers entitled to vote may vote for as many candidates as there are representatives to be elected;

(f)   the election is conducted so as to secure that –

    (i)   so far as is reasonably practicable, those voting do so in secret, and

    (ii)   the votes given at the election are fairly and accurately counted.

SCHEDULE 2 Regulations 13(4), 15(6) and 43

WORKERS EMPLOYED IN AGRICULTURE

1. Except where, in the case of a worker partly employed in agriculture, different provision is made by a relevant agreement –

(a) for the purposes of regulation 13, the leave year of a worker employed in agriculture begins on 6th April each year or such other date as may be specified in an agricultural wages order which applies to him; and

(b) the dates on which leave is taken by a worker employed in agriculture shall be determined in accordance with an agricultural wages order which applies to him.

2. Where, in the case referred to in paragraph 1 above, a relevant agreement makes provision different from sub-paragraph (a) or (b) of that paragraph –

(a) neither section 11 of the Agricultural Wages Act 1948[1] nor section 11 of the Agricultural Wages (Scotland) Act 1949[2] shall apply to that provision; and

(b) an employer giving effect to that provision shall not thereby be taken to have failed to comply with the requirements of an agricultural wages order.

3. In this Schedule, 'an agricultural wages order' means an order under section 3 of the Agricultural Wages Act 1948 or section 3 of the Agricultural Wages (Scotland) Act 1949.

1. 1948 c.47.
2. 1949 c.30.

EXPLANATORY NOTE

(This note is not part of the Regulations)

These Regulations implement Council Directive 93/104/EC concerning certain aspects of the organization of working time (OJ No L307, 13.12.93, p 18) and provisions concerning working time in Council Directive 94/33/EC on the protection of young people at work (OJ No L216, 20.8.94, p 12). The provisions in the latter Directive which are implemented relate only to adolescents (those aged between 15 and 18 who are over compulsory school age); provisions in that Directive in relation to adolescents employed on ships are to be included in separate regulations to be made shortly after the date on which these Regulations are made, and adolescents employed on ships are accordingly excluded from the scope of these Regulations (regulation 26).

Regulations 4 to 9 in these Regulations impose obligations on employers, enforceable by the Health and Safety Executive and local authorities; failure to comply is an offence. The obligations concern the maximum average weekly working time of workers (subject to provisions for individual workers to agree that the maximum should not apply to them), the average normal hours of night workers, the provision of health assessments for night workers, and rest breaks to be given to workers engaged in certain kinds of work; employers are also required to keep record of workers' hours of work.

Regulations 10 to 17 confer rights on workers, enforceable by proceedings before employment tribunals. The rights are to a rest period in every 24 hours during which a worker works for his employer and longer rest periods each week or fortnight, to a rest break in the course of a working day, and to a period of paid annual leave.

Regulations 18 to 27 provide for particular regulations not to apply, either in relation to workers engaged in certain kinds of work or where particular circumstances arise. There is also provision for groups of workers and their employers to agree to modify or exclude the application of particular regulations.

The remaining regulations make provision in relation to enforcement and remedies, and in respect of agency workers, Crown servants, Parliamentary staff, the police, trainees and agricultural workers. The Employment Rights Act 1996 is amended to include a right for workers not to be subjected to any detriment for refusing to comply with a requirement contrary to these Regulations or to forgo a right conferred by them, and to provide that the dismissal of an employee on account of any such refusal is unfair dismissal for the purposes of that Act.

Index

48 hour rule
agreements to exclude 48 hour
  limit   5.11, 5.12
  dismissal for failure to enter into
    agreement   5.15
  duration   5.13
  effect of   5.14
  pressure to enter   5.15
  record-keeping requirements   5.11, 5.12
  termination of agreement   5.13
  unfair dismissal   5.15
amending reference period   5.6
average hours worked
  calculating   5.7
  within particular period   5.3
calculations   5.5–5.9
compliance   5.4
employer's duties   5.4
enforcement   5.4
example calculations   5.9
excluded days   5.8, 5.9
individual agreements disapplying limit   5.4
maximum weekly working time   5.3
reference period   5.3, 5.5
  amending   5.6
variation of contract   5.4
Abroad working   4.9
ACAS   7.33
Advisory Conciliation and Arbitration
Service (ACAS)   7.33
Agency workers   2.23
Agreement, relevant   4.11
  collective agreement – see Collective
    agreement
  compensatory rest   6.20
  definition   6.6
  entering into   6.6
  excluding of modifying limits   6.1
  forms   6.1
  individual agreements – see Individual
    agreements
  maximum working week, excluding
    availability   5.10
    dismissal for failure to enter into   5.15
    duration of agreement   5.13
    effect of   5.14
    employer's obligations   5.11
    pressure to enter   5.15
    record-keeping obligations   5.11, 5.12
    termination of agreement   5.13
    unfair dismissal   5.15
  meaning   6.1
  night work   5.18, 5.40
  possible exclusions or modifications   6.6
  purpose   6.6

Agreement, relevant – continued
  reference period, amendment of   5.6
  types   6.1
  which agreement to use   6.2
  workforce agreement – see Workforce
    agreement
Agricultural workers   2.30
  annual leave   5.61, 5.69
Annual leave
  agricultural workers   5.61, 5.69
  amount of remuneration   5.75
  bank holidays   5.63
  complexity of provisions   5.58
  continuous employment requirement   5.64
  dates on which leave may be taken   5.67
  determining week's pay   5.72
  entitlement   5.43, 5.58
  excluded workers   5.59
  failure to provide entitlement   5.70
  giving notice   5.68
  leave years   5.60
  new workers   5.64
  no normal hours, workers with   5.77
  notice of   5.67, 5.68
  overtime   5.73
  part-time workers   5.66
  pay   5.71
  pay in lieu of leave   5.62
  period of   5.58
  piece workers   5.76
  provisions   5.58
  public holidays   5.63
  requirements   5.58
  rest period, interaction of
    entitlement to   5.44
  shift workers   5.74
  termination of employment   5.78, 5.79
  transitional period   5.58
  week, meaning of   5.65
Appeals
  Employment Tribunals   7.30
Armed Forces
  Employment Tribunals, complaints to   7.12
  exceptions from Regulations   3.21
  exclusions from Regulations   3.2, 3.3
  members of   2.26
  young workers   3.21
Average hours worked
  example calculations
    maximum weekly working time   5.9
    night work   5.26
  maximum weekly working time
    calculating   5.7
    example calculations   5.9
    excluded days   5.8, 5.9

Average hours worked – continued
night work
  calculating   5.25
  example calculations   5.26
Baggage handlers   3.10
Bank holidays
  annual leave   5.63
Breaks – *see Rest breaks; Rest periods;*
  Weekly rest periods
Business on his/her own account test   2.11

Civil Protection Services
  exclusions from Regulations   3.2, 3.3
Collective agreements   6.7
  See also Agreement, relevant
  definition   6.7
  independent trade union   6.7
  rest breaks   5.55
  use   6.7
  workforce agreements and   6.11
Company, services through   2.21
Compensation
  Employment Tribunals   7.20
  heads of   7.15
Compensatory rest   6.20
Compliance with Regulations
  cost of   1.8
Composition of workforce   2.1
Compromise agreements   7.34
Confidentiality   7.36
Continuity of service or production
  exceptions from Regulations   3.14, 3.17
Continuous employment requirement
  annual leave   5.64
Contracting out of statutory rights   7.35
Contracts of employment
  excluding or modifying entitlements   6.6
Control test   2.6
Crown employment   2.25
Customer contracts   2.19

Delegation, power of workers   2.18
Detriment, right not to suffer   7.17, 7.18
  remedies for suffering   7.23
  time limit for claim   7.25
Dismissal
  maximum working week, failure to
    enter into agreement excluding   5.15
  unfair – *see Unfair dismissal*
Display screen equipment   1.3
Doctors in training
  exclusions from Regulations   3.2, 3.4, 3.8
Domestic servants
  domestic servants   3.12
  entitlements   3.12
  exceptions from Regulations   3.12
  exclusions from Regulations   3.12
  health assessment   3.12
  hours of work per week   3.12
  night work   3.12, 5.30

Domestic servants – continued
  private households   3.12
  rest periods   3.12
  transfer of night worker to
    day work   3.12
DTI Guidance
  workers   2.17
Economic issues
  work patterns   1.2
Employee representatives
  election   6.9
  eligible employees   6.15
  excluding candidates   6.16
  number of   6.14
  protection of workers standing for   6.17
  purpose of election   6.18
  right not to suffer detriment   7.17
  voting rights   6.19
  workforce agreements   6.9
Employees
  See also Workers
  balance of factors   2.16
  business on his/her own
    account test   2.11
  control test   2.6
  Crown Employment   2.25
  definition   2.5
  integration test   2.7
  meaning   2.5
  multiple test   2.12
  mutual obligation   2.9
  on call   4.3
  payment   2.14
  personal service test   2.10
  premises, attendance at certain   2.15
  representatives – *see Employee*
    representatives
  self-employment and   2.11
  terms of contract   2.13
  tests to decide whether   2.5, 2.16
    balance of factors   2.16
    business on his/her own
      account test   2.11
    control test   2.6
    generally   2.5
    integration test   2.7
    multiple test   2.12
    mutual obligation   2.9
    payment   2.14
    personal service test   2.10
    premises, attendance at certain   2.15
    self-employment and   2.11
    terms of contract   2.13
    tools and equipment   2.8
  tools and equipment   2.8
Employer
  definition   2.31
  duty
    health and safety of workers, to ensure 1.3

Employer – continued
offences   7.6
  See also Offences
penalties   7.7
Employment Tribunals
  Advisory Conciliation and
    Arbitration Service (ACAS)   7.33
  appeals   7.30
  Armed Forces   7.12
  compensation   7.20
    heads of   7.15
  complaint, worker's   7.10
  compromise agreements   7.34
  conciliation of claims   7.32
  contracting out of statutory rights   7.35
  enforcement by   7.9
  fixed term contracts   7.20
  holiday pay   7.16
  mitigation of loss   7.23
  out of time complaints   7.13
  perceived rights or entitlements   7.21
  remedies   7.14, 7.22
  termination of employment   7.19
  time limits for bringing claim   7.11
  unfair dismissal – *see Unfair dismissal*
  worker's complaint   7.10
Enforcement of Regulations
  civil courts, claims in   7.1, 7.31
  conciliation   7.32
  confidentiality   7.36
  contracting out of statutory rights   7.35
  Employment Tribunals – *see*
    Employment Tribunals
  Health and Safety Executive
    basis for enforcement   7.2
    generally   7.1
    Inspector's powers   7.4, 7.5
    responsibility   7.2
    restrictions on Inspector's powers   7.5
    scope of enforcing powers   7.3
  Inspector's powers   7.4, 7.5
  local authorities
    basis for enforcement   7.2
    generally   7.1
    Inspector's powers   7.4, 7.5
    responsibility   7.2
    scope of enforcing powers   7.3
  maximum weekly working time   5.3
  methods   7.1
  public interest disclosure   7.36
  restrictions on Inspector's powers   7.5
  scope of enforcing powers   7.3
European Commission
  report on workings of Directive   1.8
European Directives   1.6
  See also Working Time Directive
Exceptions from Regulations   3.11
  Armed Forces   3.21
  continuity of service or
    production   3.14, 3.17

Exceptions from Regulations – continued
  derogations from Directive   3.11
  domestic servants   3.12
  force majeure   3.14, 3.19
  generally   3.1
  maximum weekly working time   5.3
  night work   5.30
  re-examination of derogations   3.11
  security activities   3.14, 3.16
  ships, young workers employed on   3.20
  special cases   3.14
  surges of activity in work   3.14, 3.18
  surveillance activities   3.14, 3.16
  travelling long distance to work   3.14, 3.15
  unmeasured working time, workers on   3.13
Excessive cumulative fatigue   1.2
Exclusions from Regulations   3.2–3.10
  Armed Forces   3.2, 3.3
  baggage handlers   3.10
  basic rule   3.2
  Civil Protection Services   3.2, 3.3
  determining scope   3.9, 3.10
  doctors in training   3.2, 3.4, 3.8
  domestic servants   3.12
  future of   3.6
  generally   3.1, 3.2
  Guidance   3.10
  involvement in excluded sector,
    determining   3.10
  medical practitioners   3.4
  mobile workers   3.9
  public and private sectors, application
    of Regulations to   3.2
  review by European Commission   3.6
  scope   3.9
  seafarers   3.7
  unmeasured working time,
    workers on   3.13
  young workers   3.5
Executive, Health and Safety – *see*
  Enforcement of Regulations

Fatigue
  excessive cumulative fatigue   1.2
  research into   1.2
Fixed term contracts
  Employment Tribunals   7.20
Force majeure   3.14, 3.19
Freelance workers   2.17
Full-time employees

Health assessment
  adult workers   5.31
  carrying out   5.33
  cost   5.31
  disclosing results   5.35
  domestic servants   3.12
  free   5.31
  frequency   5.31, 5.34
  guidance   5.33

Health assessment – continued
intervals   5.31, 5.34
medical conditions exacerbated
  by night work   5.33
minimum standard   5.33
nature of   5.33
night work   5.31
purpose   5.33
questionnaire   5.33
results, disclosing   5.35
screening questionnaire   5.33
special cases   3.14
transfer of night worker to
  day work   5.36
unmeasured working time,
  workers on   3.13
young workers   5.32, 5.33, 5.39
Health and safety
employer's duty to ensure   1.3
Executive – *see Enforcement of*
  Regulations
night work   5.17
research   1.2
VDU operators   1.3
Holiday pay
See also Annual leave
Employment Tribunals   7.16
Home workers   2.17
Home, working from   4.6
Hours of work per week – *see Maximum*
  weekly working time
House of Commons staff   2.28
House of Lords staff   2.27

Implementation of Working Time
Directive   1.9
consultation on   1.9
Indemnities   2.21
Individual agreement
duration   6.3
nature of   6.3
notice to terminate   6.4
terminating   6.4
use   6.3
Integration test   2.7
International Labour Office
research on work patterns   1.2
International workers   2.2

Leave
annual – *see Annual leave*
paid – *see Paid leave*
Local authority enforcement – *see*
  Enforcement of Regulations
Long working hours
health, effect on   1.2
scientific data on   1.2
Lunch
breaks   4.4
working   4.4

Maximum weekly working time
48 hour rule   5.3
  See also 48 Hour Rule
agreement to exclude   5.10
  dismissal for not entering into   5.15
  duration of agreement   5.13
  effect of   5.14
  pressure to enter into   5.15
  record-keeping requirement   5.11, 5.12
  termination   5.13
  unfair dismissal   5.15
amendment of reference period   5.6
average hours worked
  calculating   5.7
  excluded days   5.8
  within particular period   5.3
basic rule   5.3
calculating   5.5
collective agreements   5.10
compliance   5.3, 5.4
employer's obligations   5.11
enforcement   5.3
exceptions from Regulations   5.3
excluded days   5.8
IDS Study   5.3
impact of rules   5.3
individual agreements disapplying
  limit   5.4, 5.10
other employers, work for   5.16
overtime   5.3
record-keeping requirements   5.11
reference period   5.3, 5.5
  amendment   5.6
  remuneration and   5.4
seafarers   3.7
second jobs   5.16
variation of contract   5.4
Medical practitioners
exclusions from Regulations   3.4
Mitigation of loss   7.23
Multiple test   2.12
Mutual obligation
employees   2.9

National Traineeships   2.24
New Deal   2.24
New workers
annual leave   5.64
Night work
agreement, relevant   5.18, 5.40
average length of   5.25
calculating average for   5.25
  examples   5.26
definition of night time   5.18
domestic servants   3.12, 5.30
example calculations   5.26
exceptions from Regulations   5.30
guidance   5.19
health assessments   5.31
health and safety   5.17

Night work – continued
limit on 5.22
modification of provisions 5.18, 5.40
night time 5.18
night worker 5.18
normal hours 5.24
'on call' workers 5.21
overtime 5.24
provisions relating to 5.17
record-keeping obligations 5.41
reduction in pay 5.28
reference period 5.20, 5.23
research into 5.17
rotating shift patterns 5.19
seafarers 3.7
special cases 3.14, 5.30
special hazards 5.27, 5.29
transfer of night worker to
day work
  – see *Transfer of night worker to*
  day work
unfair dismissal 5.28
unmeasured working time,
workers on 3.13, 5.30
Normal hours
night work 5.24
Northern Ireland, implementation of
Directive in 2.2

Offences
employer 7.6
fines 7.7, 7.8
penalties 7.7
prosecutions 7.8
'On call' workers 4.3
night work 5.21
Other employers, work for
maximum weekly working time 5.16
Outside Great Britain, workers 2.2
Overseas workers 2.2, 4.9
Overtime
48 hour rule 5.3
annual leave 5.73
maximum weekly working time 5.3
night work 5.24
unpaid 4.2
working time 4.2

Paid leave
See also *Annual leave*
seafarers 3.7
special cases 3.14
Part-time workers
annual leave 5.66
Patterns of work
economic issues 1.2
excessive cumulative fatigue 1.2
health, effect of 1.2
provisions 5.42
studies on 1.2

Pay
See also *Remuneration*
annual leave
  pay for 5.71
  pay in lieu of 5.62
employees 2.14
rest breaks, for 5.57
working time 4.2
Personal service test 2.10
Piece workers
annual leave 5.76
Police service workers 2.29
Public holidays
annual leave 5.63
Public interest disclosure 7.36

Questionnaire
health assessment 5.33

Reading, work-related 4.7
Record-keeping requirements
agreements to exclude 48 hour
  limit 5.11, 5.12
  duration of agreement 5.13
basic rule 4.12
maximum weekly working time 5.11
night work 5.41
seafarers 3.7
working time 4.12
Reduction in pay
night work 5.28
Reference period
maximum weekly working time 5.3, 5.5
  agreement, relevant 5.6
  amending 5.6
  annual leave during 5.8
  example calculations 5.9
  excluded days 5.8
  sickness 5.8
night work 5.20, 5.23
Regulations
enforcement – see *Enforcement of*
  Regulations
exceptions – see *Exceptions from*
  Regulations
exclusions – see *Exclusions from*
  Regulations
scope 2.1–2.31
workers, definition of 2.4
Relevant agreements 6.2
See also *Agreement, relevant; Collective*
  agreement; Individual agreement;
  Workforce agreement
Remedies
Employment Tribunals 7.14
suffering detriment 7.22
unfair dismissal 7.29
Remuneration
See also Pay 5.75
annual leave 5.75

Remuneration – continued
maximum weekly working time and 5.4
Reserve Forces, members of 2.26
Rest breaks
collective agreements 5.55
entitlement 5.52
health and safety provisions 5.52
leaving workstation 5.54
length of working day 5.52
meaning 5.54
nature of break 5.52
pay for 5.57
taking 5.53, 5.54
when to take 5.53
where to take 5.54
workforce agreements 5.55
young workers 5.56
Rest period
annual leave, interaction of
entitlement to 5.44
calculations 5.49
denying 5.43
domestic servants 3.12
economic issues 1.2
eleven hour requirement 5.46
entitlement 5.43, 5.45
excessive cumulative fatigue 1.2
interaction of entitlement to
annual leave 5.44
length 5.46
not taking 5.43
provisions 5.46
seafarers 3.7
shift workers 5.47, 5.51
special cases 3.14
special hazards 5.27
unmeasured working time,
workers on 3.13
weekly – *see Weekly rest periods*
work organisational reasons 5.44
working time 4.2
young workers 5.45, 5.46, 5.50
Right not to suffer detriment
compensation 7.24
'detriment' 7.18
employee representatives 7.17
remedies 7.22
Rights, workers 5.1–5.79
annual leave – *see Annual leave*
generally 5.1
maximum weekly working time 5.3
See also Maximum weekly working time
night work – *see Night work*
obligations upon employers 5.2
patterns of work – *see Patterns of work*
rest breaks – *see Rest breaks*
rest period – *see Rest periods*
weekly rest periods – *see Weekly rest periods*
Rotating shift patterns
night work 5.19

Sandwich courses 2.24
Scope of Regulations 2.1-2.31
See also Employees; Workers
composition of workforce 2.1
control test 2.6
employees 2.5–2.16
See also Employees
to whom do the Regulations apply 2.1
See also Employees; Workers
Seafarers
exclusions from Regulations 3.7
ILO Agreement 3.7
maximum hours 3.7
night work 3.7
paid leave 3.7
records, compliance 3.7
Second jobs
maximum weekly working time 5.16
Security activities
exceptions from Regulations 3.14, 3.16
Self-employment 2.11
arm's length relationships 2.20
test for 2.20
workers 2.20
Services through a company 2.21
Shift workers
annual leave 5.74
definition 5.47
rest period 5.47, 5.51
Ships
See also Seafarers
young workers 3.20
Sickness
reference period, during 5.8
Special cases
exceptions from Regulations 3.14
health assessment 3.14
night work 3.14, 5.30
paid leave 3.14
rest period 3.14
Special hazards
meaning 5.29
night work 5.27, 5.29
rest period 5.27
Split shifts
weekly rest periods 5.48
Surges of activity in work 3.14
exceptions from Regulations 3.14, 3.18
Surveillance activities
exceptions from Regulations 3.14, 3.16

Taking work home 4.6
Teleworkers 2.17
Termination of employment
annual leave 5.78, 5.79
Employment Tribunals, complaint to 7.19
Terms of contract
employees, status of 2.13
Tools and equipment
employees 2.8

Trade union activities   4.8
Trainees   2.24
  See also Training
  National Traineeships   2.24
  New Deal   2.24
  relevant training   2.24
  sandwich courses   2.24
Training
  See also Trainees
  relevant   2.24, 4.10
  working time   4.2, 4.10
Transfer of night worker to day work   3.12
  disability discrimination   5.36
  duty   5.36
  employers, difficulties for   5.36
  failure to find alternative work   5.37
  health assessment   5.36
  re-training workers   5.36
  reasonable adjustments   5.38
Transfer of undertakings   6.9
Travelling long distance to work   3.14
  exceptions from Regulations   3.14, 3.15
Travelling time
  working time   4.5
Tribunals – *see Employment Tribunals*

Unfair dismissal
  assertion of statutory right   7.27, 7.29
  automatic   7.26
  Employment Tribunals, complaint to   7.25
  maximum working week, failure to
    enter into agreement to exclude
    provisions   5.15
  night work   5.28
  remedies   7.30
  statutory right, assertion of   7.27, 7.29
  time limit   7.28
Unmeasured working time, workers on
  examples   3.13
  exceptions from Regulations   3.13
  exclusions from Regulations   3.13
  health assessment   3.13
  meaning   3.13
  night work   3.13, 5.30
  rest period   3.13
  scope of exception   3.13
  young workers   3.13
Unpaid overtime
  working time   4.2

Variation of contract
  48 hour rule   5.4
  consent requirement   5.4
  unilateral   5.4
VDU operators
  health and safety   1.3

Weekly rest periods
  calculations   5.49
  daily rest and   5.44

Weekly rest periods – *continued*
  entitlement   5.45, 5.48
  flexibility   5.48
  interaction of other entitlements   5.44
  split shifts   5.48
  work organisational reasons   5.44
  young workers   5.45, 5.48
Weekly working time, maximum
  – *see Maximum weekly working time*
Work patterns – *see Patterns of work*
Workers
  See also Employees
  agency   2.23
  agricultural   2.30
  Armed Forces   2.26
  casual workers   2.17
  company, services through   2.21
  conditions   2.19
  Crown employment   2.25
  customer contracts   2.19
  definition   2.1, 2.2
    Industrial Relations Act 1971   2.4
    Regulations   2.4
    Working Time Directive   2.3
  delegation, power of   2.18
  DTI Guidance   2.17
  England   2.2
  freelance   2.17
  home workers   2.17
  House of Commons staff   2.28
  House of Lords staff   2.27
  international   2.2
  night   5.19
    See also Night work
  Northern Ireland   2.2
  ordinarily working outside Great Britain   2.2
  outside Great Britain   2.2
  overseas   2.2, 4.9
  part-time, annual leave for   5.66
  place of work   2.2
  police service   2.29
  Regulations, definition in   2.4
  rights – *see Rights, workers*
  Scotland   2.2
  self-employment   2.20
  services through a company   2.21
  teleworkers   2.17
  trainees   2.24
  Wales   2.2
  Working Time Directive definition   2.3
  young – *see Young workers*
Workforce agreements
  See also Agreement, relevant
  collective agreements and   6.11
  concluding   6.9
  definition   6.8
  elected representatives   6.13
  employee representatives – *see*
    Employee representatives
  formal requirements for   6.12

Workforce agreements – continued
formalities   6.10
meaning   6.9
purpose   6.8
requirements for   6.13
rest breaks   5.55
using   6.10
Working time
abroad, working   4.9
agreement, relevant   4.11
concept of   4.1
definition   4.1, 4.2
Directive – *see Working Time Directive*
EU Member States, in   1.5
home, working from   4.6
legislation other than Regulations   1.3
lunch breaks   4.4
maximum weekly – *see Maximum
      weekly working time*
meaning   4.1
'on call' employees   4.3
overtime   4.2
payment   4.2
reading, work-related   4.7
record-keeping requirements   4.12
rest period   4.2
statistics on workers working
      longer than 48 hours   1.4, 1.5
statutory right to time off   4.8
taking work home   4.6
time off, statutory right to   4.8

Working time – continued
trade union activities   4.8
training   4.2, 4.10
travelling time   4.5
UK, in   1.4
unpaid overtime   4.2
work-related activities   4.7
Working Time Directive
cases   1.10
challenging   1.7
compatibility of Regulations
      with   1.10
consultation on implementation   1.9
cost of compliance   1.8
implementation   1.8, 1.9
interpretation   1.10
role   1.10
scope   2.3

Young workers
Armed Forces   3.21
definition of young worker   2.22
Directive   1.6, 2.22
exclusions from Regulations   3.5
health assessment   5.32, 5.33, 5.39
rest breaks   5.56
rest period   5.45, 5.46, 5.50
ships   3.20
unmeasured working time,
      workers on   3.13
weekly rest periods   5.45, 5.48